First World War
and Army of Occupation
War Diary
France, Belgium and Germany

33 DIVISION
98 Infantry Brigade
Royal Fusiliers (City of London Regiment)
21st Battalion
26 April 1916 - 31 January 1917

WO95/2427/4

The Naval & Military Press Ltd
www.nmarchive.com
Published in association with The National Archives

Published by

The Naval & Military Press Ltd

Unit 10 Ridgewood Industrial Park,

Uckfield, East Sussex,

TN22 5QE England

Tel: +44 (0) 1825 749494

www.naval-military-press.com

www.nmarchive.com

This diary has been reprinted in facsimile from the original. Any imperfections are inevitably reproduced and the quality may fall short of modern type and cartographic standards.

© **Crown Copyright**
Images reproduced by permission of The National Archives, London, England, 2015.

Contents

Document type	Place/Title	Date From	Date To
Miscellaneous	WO95/2427/5 Brig M/Gen Co. 1916 April-1918 Jan		
Heading	33rd Division 98th Infy Bde 98th Machine Gun Coy Apr 1916 Jan 1918		
Heading	98th Brigade. 33rd Division. Disembarked Havre 26.4.16. 98th Brigade Machine Gun Company 26th April to 31st May 1916 1 Jan 18		
Heading	War Diary of 98 Machine Gun Company from April 26th 1916 to May 31st 1916 Volume 1		
War Diary	Havre	26/04/1916	27/04/1916
War Diary	Bethune	28/04/1916	04/05/1916
War Diary	Beuvry	05/05/1916	31/05/1916
Heading	98th Brigade 33rd Division. 98th Brigade Machine Gun Company June 1916		
War Diary	Beuvry	01/06/1916	30/06/1916
Heading	98th Inf. Bde. 33rd Div. War Diary 98th Machine Gun Company July 1916		
War Diary	Beuvry	01/07/1916	07/07/1916
War Diary	Beuvry & Chocques	08/07/1916	08/07/1916
War Diary	Rainville	09/07/1916	10/07/1916
War Diary	Rainville Corbie	11/07/1916	11/07/1916
War Diary	Corbie Ville-Sous Corbie	12/07/1916	12/07/1916
War Diary	Ville Sous Corbie Meaulte	13/07/1916	13/07/1916
War Diary	Meaulte Fricourt	14/07/1916	14/07/1916
War Diary	Mametz Wood-Bazentin Le-Petis Wood	15/07/1916	15/07/1916
War Diary	Bazentin-Le Petit Wood & Village	16/07/1916	16/07/1916
War Diary	Bazentin-Le Petit Village & Wood	17/07/1916	18/07/1916
War Diary	Bazentin Woods	19/07/1916	21/07/1916
War Diary	Mametz Wood	21/07/1916	21/07/1916
War Diary	Mametz Wood Dernancourt	22/07/1916	22/07/1916
War Diary	Dernancourt	23/07/1916	31/07/1916
Heading	98th Brigade. 33rd Division. 98th Brigade Machine Gun Company August 1916		
War Diary	Dernancourt	01/08/1916	05/08/1916
War Diary	Dernancourt & Mametz Wood	06/08/1916	06/08/1916
War Diary	Mametz Wood	07/08/1916	12/08/1916
War Diary	Mametz Wood & High Wood	13/08/1916	13/08/1916
War Diary	High Wood	14/08/1916	18/08/1916
War Diary	High Wood & Fricourt	19/08/1916	19/08/1916
War Diary	Fricourt	20/08/1916	21/08/1916
War Diary	Fricourt Becordel	22/08/1916	22/08/1916
War Diary	Becordel	23/08/1916	24/08/1916
War Diary	Becordel Pomiers Redout	25/08/1916	25/08/1916
War Diary	Trenches	26/08/1916	30/08/1916
War Diary	Trenches Dernancourt	31/08/1916	31/08/1916
Heading	98th Brigade. 33rd Division. 98th Brigade Machine Gun Company September 1916		
War Diary	Dernancourt & Allonville	01/09/1916	01/09/1916
War Diary	Allonville & Fienvillers	02/09/1916	02/09/1916
War Diary	Fienvillers	03/09/1916	03/09/1916
War Diary	Fienvillers & Mezerolles	04/09/1916	04/09/1916

War Diary	Mezerolles & Haute Cote	05/09/1916	05/09/1916
War Diary	Haute Cote	06/09/1916	07/09/1916
War Diary	Haute Cote Warluzel	08/09/1916	08/09/1916
War Diary	Warluzel & Sus St Leger	09/09/1916	09/09/1916
War Diary	Bros St. Leger & Saulty	10/09/1916	10/09/1916
War Diary	Saulty	11/09/1916	12/09/1916
War Diary	Saulty and Humbercamp	13/09/1916	13/09/1916
War Diary	Humbercamp.	14/09/1916	18/09/1916
War Diary	Humbercamp & Bayencourt.	19/09/1916	19/09/1916
War Diary	Bayencourt & Trenches	20/09/1916	20/09/1916
War Diary	Trenches	21/09/1916	30/09/1916
Heading	98th Brigade. 33rd Division. 98th Brigade Machine Gun Company October 1916		
War Diary	Trenches at Hebuterne	01/10/1916	01/10/1916
War Diary	Sus. St. Leger	02/10/1916	18/10/1916
War Diary	Daours	19/10/1916	20/10/1916
War Diary	Meaulte	21/10/1916	23/10/1916
War Diary	Trenches Les Boeufs	24/10/1916	24/10/1916
War Diary	Trenches Les Boeufs	25/10/1916	31/10/1916
Heading	98th Brigade. 33rd Division. 98th Brigade Machine Gun Company November 1916		
Miscellaneous	To 98th Inf Bde	03/12/1916	03/12/1916
Miscellaneous	98th Inf Bde		
War Diary	Trenches	01/11/1916	02/11/1916
War Diary	Carnoy	02/11/1916	04/11/1916
War Diary	Meaulte	05/11/1916	09/11/1916
War Diary	Limeux	10/11/1916	30/11/1916
Heading	98th Brigade. 33rd Division. 98th Brigade Machine Gun Company December 1916		
Heading	War Diary Of 98th Machine Gun Company From 1-12-16- 31-12-16 Vol 8		
War Diary	Limeux	01/12/1916	04/12/1916
War Diary	Limeux Bray	05/12/1916	05/12/1916
War Diary	Bray	06/12/1916	06/12/1916
War Diary	Bray & Camp Roy	07/12/1916	07/12/1916
War Diary	Campioy	08/12/1916	08/12/1916
War Diary	Maricourt Wood	09/12/1916	09/12/1916
War Diary	Trenches	10/12/1916	18/12/1916
War Diary	Camp 17	19/12/1916	22/12/1916
War Diary	Trenches	23/12/1916	27/12/1916
War Diary	Camp 112	28/12/1916	29/12/1916
War Diary	Vauchelles-Les-Domart	30/12/1916	31/12/1916
Heading	War Diary of No. 98 Machine Gun Company From 1st January 1917 to 31st January 1917 Vol 9		
War Diary	Vauchelles Les-Domart	01/01/1917	04/01/1917
War Diary	Bettencourt St-Ouen	05/01/1917	19/01/1917
War Diary	Camp 13	20/01/1917	22/01/1917
War Diary	Suzanne	23/01/1917	23/01/1917
War Diary	Trenches	24/01/1917	27/01/1917
War Diary	Camp 19	28/01/1917	30/01/1917
War Diary	Trenches	31/01/1917	31/01/1917
Heading	War Diary of No. 98 Machine Gun Coy From 1st Feb. 1917 to 28 Feb 1917 inclusive Vol 10		
War Diary	Trenches	01/02/1917	15/02/1917
War Diary	Suzanne (Camp 1)	16/02/1917	23/02/1917
War Diary	Trenches	24/02/1917	28/02/1917

Type	Location	Start	End
Heading	War Diary of No 98 Machine Gun Coy. For March 1917 Vol XI		
War Diary	Trenches	01/03/1917	07/03/1917
War Diary	Suzanne	08/03/1917	08/03/1917
War Diary	Sailly-Laurette	09/03/1917	31/03/1917
Heading	War Diary of No. 98 Machine Gun Company from 1st to 30th April 1917 Vol 12		
War Diary	Sailly Laurette	01/04/1917	01/04/1917
War Diary	Bussy-Les-Daours	02/04/1917	02/04/1917
War Diary	Rhineville	03/04/1917	03/04/1917
War Diary	La Vicogne	04/04/1917	04/04/1917
War Diary	Gezaincourt	05/04/1917	05/04/1917
War Diary	Pommera	06/04/1917	07/04/1917
War Diary	Couin	08/04/1917	08/04/1917
War Diary	Berles-Au-Bois	09/04/1917	11/04/1917
War Diary	Blaireville	12/04/1917	12/04/1917
War Diary	Sukerrdnd 1 Mile S W of Mercatel	13/04/1917	16/04/1917
War Diary	Trenches	17/04/1917	24/04/1917
War Diary	Henin-Sur-Cojeul	25/04/1917	26/04/1917
War Diary	Bellacourt	27/04/1917	30/04/1917
War Diary	War Diary of No. 98 Machine Gun Company for the month of May 1917 Vol 13		
War Diary	Bellacourt	01/05/1917	02/05/1917
War Diary	Ayette	03/05/1917	11/05/1917
War Diary	Trenches Opp Fontaine	12/05/1917	31/05/1917
Heading	War Diary of No. 98 Machine Gun Company for the month of June 1917		
War Diary	Blaireville	01/06/1917	17/06/1917
War Diary	Blaireville & Boyelles	18/06/1917	18/06/1917
War Diary	Trenches opp Fontaine Lez-Croisilles	19/06/1917	19/06/1917
War Diary	Trenches Opp Fontaine	20/06/1917	30/06/1917
Miscellaneous	A Form. Messages And Signals.		
Heading	War Diary of No. 98 Machine Gun Company for the month of July 1917		
War Diary	Bailleuval	01/07/1917	03/07/1917
War Diary	Acheux	04/07/1917	04/07/1917
War Diary	Talmas	05/07/1917	05/07/1917
War Diary	Belloy Sur Somme	06/07/1917	06/07/1917
War Diary	Avelesges	07/07/1917	31/07/1917
Heading	War Diary of No. 98 Machine Gun Company for the month of August 1917 Vol 16		
War Diary	La Panne Bains	01/08/1917	16/08/1917
War Diary	Coxyde Al	17/08/1917	18/08/1917
War Diary	Trenches	19/08/1917	28/08/1917
War Diary	Coxyde	29/08/1917	29/08/1917
War Diary	Bray Dunes	30/08/1917	31/08/1917
Heading	War Diary of 98 Machine Gun Company for the Month of September 1917 Vol. 17		
War Diary	Bray Dunes	01/09/1917	01/09/1917
War Diary	Salperwick	02/09/1917	05/09/1917
War Diary	Watten	06/09/1917	14/09/1917
War Diary	Noropeene	15/09/1917	15/09/1917
War Diary	Steenvorde	16/09/1917	16/09/1917
War Diary	Berthen	17/09/1917	19/09/1917
War Diary	Reninghelst	20/09/1917	22/09/1917
War Diary	Railway Dugouts	23/09/1917	23/09/1917

War Diary	Trenches N.W. of Gheluvelt	24/09/1917	24/09/1917
War Diary	Trenches	25/09/1917	27/09/1917
War Diary	Railway Dugouts	28/09/1917	28/09/1917
War Diary	Ebblinghem	29/09/1917	30/09/1917
Heading	War Diary of No. 98 Machine Gun Company from 1st to 31st October 1917 Vol 18		
War Diary	Renescure	01/10/1917	05/10/1917
War Diary	Hallines	06/10/1917	06/10/1917
War Diary	Neuve Eglise	07/10/1917	23/10/1917
War Diary	Trenches Opposite Nessines	23/10/1917	28/10/1917
War Diary	Trenches Near Messines	29/10/1917	31/10/1917
Heading	War Diary of 98 Machine Gun Company for Month of November 1917 Vol 19		
War Diary	Neuve Eglise	01/11/1917	12/11/1917
War Diary	Merris	13/11/1917	16/11/1917
War Diary	Potijze	17/11/1917	19/11/1917
War Diary	Trenches Near Passchendaele	20/11/1917	22/11/1917
War Diary	Potijze	23/11/1917	26/11/1917
War Diary	1 Mile S.W. of Passchendaele	27/11/1917	30/11/1917
Heading	War Diary of 98 Machine Gun Company for Month of December 1917 Vol 20		
War Diary	Potijze	01/12/1917	03/12/1917
War Diary	Trenches S. of Passchendaele	04/12/1917	08/12/1917
War Diary	Potijze	09/12/1917	12/12/1917
War Diary	Billets Near Steenvoorde	13/12/1917	31/12/1917
Heading	War Diary of 98 M.G. Coy for the Month of January 1918 Vol 21		
War Diary	Billets Near Steenvoorde	01/01/1918	03/01/1918
War Diary	Ridge Camp Brandhoek	04/01/1918	04/01/1918
War Diary	M.G. Camp Potize	05/01/1918	09/01/1918
War Diary	Potijze	10/01/1917	12/01/1917
War Diary	Passchendaele	13/01/1917	16/01/1917
War Diary	Potijze	17/01/1917	20/01/1917
War Diary	Passchendaele	21/01/1917	24/01/1917
War Diary	Potizje	25/01/1917	27/01/1917
War Diary	Quercamp	28/01/1917	31/01/1917

WO 95 2427/5

BRIG M/GUN CO. 1916 APRIL
— 1918 JAN

33RD DIVISION
98TH INFY BDE

98TH MACHINE GUN COY
APR 1916 - JAN 1918

98th Brigade.
33rd Division.

Disembarked   Havre 26.4.16.

98th BRIGADE MACHINE GUN COMPANY

26th APRIL to 31st MAY 1916.

XXXIII
98 M G Coy
Vol 1

Confidential

War Diary
of
98 Machine Gun Company
From April 26th 1916 To May 31st 1916
Volume.

C. D. Jay Capt.
O.C. 98 M.G. Coy.

WAR DIARY
or
INTELLIGENCE SUMMARY

(Erase heading not required.)

Army Form C. 2118.

Place	Date	Hour	Summary of Events and Information	Remarks and references to Appendices
HAVRE	26/4/16		The Company arrived at HAVRE from SOUTHAMPTON at 5:30 a.m. after a good passage and boarding took place at 2:45 p.m. owing to the tide being low on arrival. Spent the night at No. 1 Rest Camp very hot and trying march.	C.D.S.
HAVRE	27/4/16		Left the rest camp at 12:30 p.m. and entrained for BETHUNE 1:50 p.m.	C.D.S.
BETHUNE	28/4/16		Arrived at BETHUNE 10:15 a.m. detrained and proceeded to the COLLEGE DES JEUNES FILLES where the Coy were billeted, the animals and limbers were parked in square belonging to the COLLEGE the Officers were billeted at a house opposite.	C.D.S.
BETHUNE	29/4/16		The Coy were inspected by Major General H.T.S. LANDON C.B. at 12:15 p.m. he afterwards addressed the officers, a rifle & foot inspection was held in the afternoon after which the Coy was paid out. Time and Piquet guards were mounted.	C.D.S.
BETHUNE	30/4/16		The inspection was carried out by Section Officers. A,B & C section paraded at 11:30 & the trenches for instruction. Division paraded to the trenches 1:45 A & B sections attacked the 2nd ROYAL WARWICKS in the CUINCHY sector, C section to the 1/6 SCOTTISH RIFLES and D section to the 1/6 K.R.R. in the AUCHY sector. The G.S. waggon with drivers attached to No 2 Coy A.S.C. from this date.	C.D.S.
BETHUNE	1/5/16		The section Officers and Coy to the trenches under instruction. Transport carried on exercise and at 7 p.m. took rations at the HARLEY STREET for use in the trenches.	C.D.S.
BETHUNE	2/5/16		Coy in the trenches for instruction. All quiet.	C.D.S.
BETHUNE	3/5/16		Coy in the trenches for instruction. Guns cleaned. Relieving party proceeded to BEUVRY and carried to Coy billets. A,B,& D sections arrived back from the trenches 8:50 p.m. C section at 12:15 a.m. 4th inst. 3554 Pte. The village shelled in action and 10859 Pte. SANSONI wounded (suffering from shock), Relit any direct hit on a dug out by enemy 20cm. Gun in AUCHY SECTOR	C.D.S.

WAR DIARY
or
INTELLIGENCE SUMMARY
(Erase heading not required.)

Army Form C. 2118.

Place	Date	Hour	Summary of Events and Information	Remarks and references to Appendices
BETHUNE	4/5/16		The Coy had baths from 9 a.m. to 10 a.m. The remainder of the morning after cleaning billets and feeding civvies parades as defaulters at BEUVRY. Coy left BETHUNE 3 p.m. and arrived at billets 4:30 p.m. Coy billeted in buses and lorries at RUE DE SAIL, BEUVRY. Coy M.G's were handed over to 98 Bde who proceeded to the trenches.	Q.M.S.
BEUVRY	5/5/16		Coy received a lecture on discipline at 8:30 a.m. {A.B.C.D. sections} 1 officer and 12 men per section proceeded to the trenches at 9:30 to take charge of guns already in position. The remainder of the Coy was paid and in the afternoon. 1000 rounds fired from gun at N1 during the course of the night. (civilians) All quiet.	Q.M.S.
BEUVRY	6/5/16		Rifle inspection and other parade during the morning. All quiet in the line. Lieut ATHERTON admitted to No 7 General Hospital MALASSISE suffering from GERMAN MEASLES Indirect gun from N1 carried on throughout the night.	Q.M.S.
BEUVRY	7/5/16		1 officer and 48 men relieved in the trenches by the other half of the Coy during the morning. All quiet. Indirect fire laid on AUCHY at intervals throughout the night.	Q.M.S.
BEUVRY	8/5/16		All quiet. Effects noticed on enemy movements between 6 & 9.2 gun fired ten rounds from railway line. Wave of firing detected at 6.15 a.m. 32 gun at N1 (indirect fire position) was put out of action owing to the cover of the ammunition standing. A spare gun was immediately sent up to replace the damaged one.	Q.M.S.
BEUVRY	9/5/16		Early morning parades march and double. Half Coy in trenches relieved by other half Coy during the morning. All quiet in the line.	Q.M.S.
BEUVRY	10/5/16		Early morning parade, march & double. Lectures on discipline. To Coy bathed in the morning. Physical drill, inspection of feet & equipment during the afternoon. 12" How fired from Beuvre billets time. 30 rounds 6 p.m. onwards. All quiet in the line.	Q.M.S.

Army Form C. 2118.

WAR DIARY
or
INTELLIGENCE SUMMARY
(Erase heading not required.)

Instructions regarding War Diaries and Intelligence Summaries are contained in F. S. Regs., Part II. and the Staff Manual respectively. Title Pages will be prepared in manuscript.

Place	Date	Hour	Summary of Events and Information	Remarks and references to Appendices
BEUVRY	11.5.16		Relief of ½ Coy in the trenches by the other ½ Coy. 20 men & 4 N.C.O's of 4th King's and 20 men & 4 N.C.O's of ¼ Suffolk T. Regt. attached to the Coy from this date. 20288 the HALL H. of 4th King's Regt. wounded by shell fire at 6 P.M. in the trenches, otherwise all quiet	25.8.
BEUVRY	12.5.16		Inspection & overhaul of ½ limbers. the rest of the morning all quiet in the line.	25.8.
BEUVRY	13.5.16		Relief of ½ Coy in the trenches by other ½ Coy. ½ day cleaning up billets. all quiet in the line	25.8.
BEUVRY	14.5.16		Small Calibre shells by Section officers in the morning. ½ Coy in billets attended Divine Service in the R.E. Canteen 11:30 A.M. all quiet in the line. Gun fired on GERMAN SUPPORT LINES throughout the night all quiet. Indirect fire on AUCHY & RLY TRIANGLE	D.S.
BEUVRY	15.5.16		Instruction in BARR & STROUD during morning. (B Section gun) INDIRECT FIRE HOUSE carried out in the latter order owing to the connecting rod breaking. Another gun sent immediately to take its place. all quiet. 8990 Pte IKING W located in place all quiet.	25.8.
BEUVRY	16.5.16		Usual parades throughout the day. Coy found one in afternoon. Became all quiet in the line. 2nd Lieut ATHERTON returned to duty	25.8.
BEUVRY	17.5.16		Relief of gun teams in the trenches A maxim gun drawn in. faces of guns over & action. all quiet in the line. Indirect fire on LABASSEE ROAD & AUCHY	D.S.
BEUVRY	18.5.16		Instruction to section on MAXIM GUN. 11308 Pte ENSOR D & 13469 Pte BEGLEY by shell fire 10 am morning. otherwise all quiet.	25.8.
BEUVRY	19.5.16		Physical drill & musks faults instruction on MAXIM continued. all quiet. '13478 Pte HIGGINS obtained his Leaving will 20.5.16.	25.8.
BEUVRY	20.5.16		Main Dugout carried in the morning 2ⁿᵈLieut GILL C.A. & 26532 Pte RIDDING Rifle Grenade BRICKSTACK 10 wounded by	25.8.

2449 Wt. W14957/M90 750,000 1/16 J.B.C. & A. Forms/C.2118/12.

WAR DIARY
or
INTELLIGENCE SUMMARY

(Erase heading not required.)

Army Form C. 2118.

Instructions regarding War Diaries and Intelligence Summaries are contained in F. S. Regs., Part II and the Staff Manual respectively. Title Pages will be prepared in manuscript.

No. 88 MACHINE GUN COY. MACHINE GUN CORPS

Place	Date	Hour	Summary of Events and Information	Remarks and references to Appendices
BEUVRY	21/5/16		Relief by 4th Coy in afternoon of 88th Coy in trenches. Rifle Grenades from enemy on BRICKSTACK 12 and WINDMILL action. Watermelons burst in afternoon. Waded on entrance in the line.	2 & 5
BEUVRY	22/5/16		Usual parades. Pte. HIGGINS discharged from Service. Unden overhauled. All quiet in the line.	2 & 5
BEUVRY	23/5/16		Parades as usual. During the night M.G. emplacements made on RAILWAY EMBANKMENT for trench by 2.45 was also an emplacement at TOWER & REVETRENCH all guns. S/722 Sergt. BEARD & KING'S proceeded on Rennie Gun artillery action shelling enemy from line 4 p.m. MG fire at 10.30	2 & 5
BEUVRY	24/5/16		Parades as usual. At 12.15 artillery in conjunction with 4 Machine Guns firing to our front fire bombarded German front line 150° south of LA BASSÉE ROAD in rifts of casting machine fire for damage done 4 p.m. 23rd night. Gun was again retired at 2,300 m Germans action throughout all day with heavy machine and rifle grenades. One of our mines was fired at 12 midnight. This caused retaliation on part of Germans.	2 & 5
BEUVRY	25/5/16		Parades during the morning. 2nd Coy relieved in the trenches by 1st Coy in evening. Pte TEAR admitted to Enfield Sick. Six Germans succeeded in the trenches for machine action all quiet.	2 & 5
BEUVRY	26/5/16		Parades in 2,000 as usual. All quiet in the line. Indians fire enemy trenches during the night.	2 & 5
BEUVRY	27/5/16		PUSSEGLEY & ENSOR wounded. 18t wagt returned to duty. All quiet in the line.	2 & 5
BEUVRY	28/5/16		Church Parade for men in 2,000, 12 noon. Pte HOPE A.S.C. Remit on attached. Received orders for relief by 116th M G Coy at 2.30 p.m. Afterwoods cleaning & packing returned at 7 p.m. Red & in moon motorbus and got there C.H.H. GOTLEY.	2 & 5

2449 Wt. W14957/M90 750,000 1/16 J.B.C. & A. Forms/C.2118/12.

WAR DIARY
or
INTELLIGENCE SUMMARY

(Erase heading not required.)

Army Form C. 2118.

Instructions regarding War Diaries and Intelligence Summaries are contained in F. S. Regs., Part II. and the Staff Manual respectively. Title Pages will be prepared in manuscript.

Place	Date	Hour	Summary of Events and Information	Remarks and references to Appendices
BEUVRY	28/5/16 contd.		in charge of 116th M.G. Coy. This Coy had we been in trenches before or 2 officers and one man too gun left in the trenches to instruct the new comers. Relief reported complete 6.30 a.m. 29th. Remand over reliefs escort mofa ete Coy in 2nd Left & L m N. BEUVRY	N.BEUVRY
BEUVRY	29/5/16		Excercised in man Rifles overalls, Everhauling & cleaning & guns cleaning up generally. Little Rifle in trenches returned 11 a.m. all correct.	S.R.S.
BEUVRY	30/5/16		Under orders to move off this Comm. Relieved. Unmolested during afternoon. Inspection of Iron rations, rifles, Helmets, and Kit.	S.R.S
BEUVRY	31/5/16		Under orders to move from Communities. Comm order cancelled. Warned parade. Lieut TRENEMAN. W.K. transferred from GRANTHAM at this date. 27072 Pte HALL W. J. 14583 Pte PILKINGTON.P.A. 14549 Pte MOORE. R. taken on the strength of this day from ESTAPLES on the date. No other casualties.	S.R.S.

2449 Wt. W14957/M90 750,000 1/16 J.B.C. & A. Forms/C.2118/12.

98th Brigade,
33rd Division.

98th BRIGADE MACHINE GUN COMPANY

JUNE 1916

WAR DIARY or INTELLIGENCE SUMMARY

Army Form C. 2118.

Place	Date	Hour	Summary of Events and Information	Remarks and references to Appendices
BEUVRY	1/6/16		Parades as usual throughout the day. Route march carrying guns during the morning. Coy had Bath in the afternoon. Coy in rest billets.	Q.M.S.
BEUVRY	2/6/16		Parades as usual. The G.O.C. came round during the morning & saw the mens billets and visited stores in small Q.M. drill.	Q.M.S.
BEUVRY	3/6/16		Parades as usual throughout the morning. The Coy inspected at 3.0 p.m. by General STRICKLAND. G.O.C. 98th BRIGADE. 14 N.C.O.s and men on parade. 10 officers	Q.M.S.
BEUVRY	4/6/16		The Coy attended Divine Service in the Cinema Hall BEUVRY. No parades in company.	Q.M.S.
BEUVRY	5/6/16		Training continued. Tactical schemes out getting throughout the day.	Q.M.S.
BEUVRY	6/6/16		Parades as usual, gun drills and overhauling guns. Duties and march throughout afternoon.	Q.M.S.
BEUVRY	7/6/16		Coy on the Range during the morning. All ranks did 25 rounds practice. The G.O.C. came round during the afternoon & saw the men at firing.	Q.M.S.
BEUVRY	8/6/16		Parades as usual. Coy paid into the afternoon. Main billet to Bomb Stores RUE de BAL BEUVRY. in the evening.	Q.M.S.
BEUVRY	9/6/16		Training continued. Gun drills, squad drills & range taking.	Q.M.S.
BEUVRY	10/6/16		Parades as usual. Company went to OBLINGHEM to have showers & get clean clothes during the afternoon.	Q.M.S.
BEUVRY	11/6/16		Coy relieved 116 M.G. Coy in CUINCHY Sector. Relief completed 3 a.m. All quiet throughout the day. Gun drills & cleaning of guns in the afternoon.	Q.M.S.
BEUVRY	12/6/16		All quiet in the line, trenches in a very bad state owing to continuous rain. Several guns left at Machinegun Officers Dugout.	Q.M.S.

Army Form C. 2118.

WAR DIARY
or
INTELLIGENCE SUMMARY
(Erase heading not required.)

Instructions regarding War Diaries and Intelligence Summaries are contained in F. S. Regs., Part II. and the Staff Manual respectively. Title Pages will be prepared in manuscript.

No. 98 MACHINE GUN COY. — MACHINE GUN CORPS.

Place	Date	Hour	Summary of Events and Information	Remarks and references to Appendices
BEUVRY	13/6/16		Single shells & general shelling of the BRICKSTACKS throughout the day. No damage done. Rain continuous. 2 Officers and 2. O. R. sent to course of instruction to HQ & O C	A.9.8
BEUVRY	14/6/16		All quiet in the morning. At 2.30 P.M. an an 8.00 a.m. the enemy retaliated at and 28,000 rounds 50 places of cutting our wire frontage, were fired. Enemy retaliated with other forms at same period. All clear observed on Guns in AUCHY SECTION same at 11 P.M. Total casualties of 29. O. R. sent to the course on 13/6/16	A.9.8
BEUVRY	15/6/16		Intermittent shelling of ridge zone S. of LABASSÉE CANAL. Also outside S. Trench mortar activity. Pickets fixed up by enemy at AUCHY CROSS ROADS and German communication trenches. Remainder of night quiet.	A.9.8
BEUVRY	16/6/16		M.m guns relieved by M.m guns of the 100 M.G. Coy. Single activity in enemy wire, throughout the day. Rifle enfilade on O.P.M.	A.9.8
BEUVRY	17/6/16		The Company relieved the 19th M.G. Coy in the GIVENCHY SECTOR, and the trenches being the remainder of the Coy marched over 2600 rounds from the 22nd M.G. Coy R.E. in Le PRÉOL. All quiet on our trenches in a bad state.	A.9.8
BEUVRY	18/6/16		All quiet in our section. Fired from various points throughout the night at GERMAN communication trenches.	A.9.8
BEUVRY	19/6/16		All quiet in the day and fired throughout the night by indirect enfilade command of and enfilade command in rear lines.	A.9.8
BEUVRY	20/6/16		Four guns relieved by 19 M.G. Coy in the trenches by 195 M.G. Coy 4 guns and rest to attack 15 100 M.G. Coy in CUINCHY SECTOR, all quiet in the lines	A.9.8
BEUVRY	21/6/16		Remainder of the Coy relieved in the trenches by 195 M.G. Coy. The Coy moved back to Roman billets in RUE DE BAL BEUVRY	A.9.8

Army Form C. 2118.

WAR DIARY
or
INTELLIGENCE SUMMARY

(Erase heading not required.)

Instructions regarding War Diaries and Intelligence Summaries are contained in F. S. Regs., Part II. and the Staff Manual respectively. Title Pages will be prepared in manuscript.

Place	Date	Hour	Summary of Events and Information	Remarks and references to Appendices
BEUVRY	22/6/16		The remains of occupied in cleaning up, guns overhauled and emplacements inspection Route march	27.58
BEUVRY	23/6/16		Training continued. McCannon lectures on field message etc.	23.58
BEUVRY	24/6/16		Usual parades. Every man attending 60 day. Company voluntary concert at 6 P.M. in cinema hall in BEUVRY Coy Concert at 6 p.m. in Cinema Hall	24.58
BEUVRY	25/6/16		Coy attended Divine Service in CINEMA HALL BEUVRY. Summons & sports in the afternoon	25.58
BEUVRY	26/6/16		Usual parades in ordre. Bayonet fighting and camouflage. Also practice with dusk gas helmets	26.58
BEUVRY	27/6/16		Brigade Route March in the morning. Route GORE LE HAMEL ESSARS BEUVRY. Gas inspection in the afternoon	27.58
BEUVRY	28/6/16		Usual parades. Rainy throughout day. Weather bad	28.58
BEUVRY	29/6/16		Tactical schemes carried out on ridge S.W. of BETHUNE. Ground covered with numerous trenches.	29.58
BEUVRY	30/6/16		Route March in the morning. Company Parade out in the afternoon after parade	30.58

P. C. [signature] Capt.
Commanding No. 98 M. G. Coy.

98th Inf.Bde.
33rd Div.

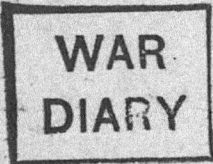

98th MACHINE GUN COMPANY.

J U L Y

1 9 1 6

Army Form C. 2118

July
33
Vol 3

WAR DIARY or INTELLIGENCE SUMMARY

(Erase heading not required.)

Place	Date	Hour	Summary of Events and Information	Remarks and references to Appendices
BEUVRY.	1.7.16.		Usual trench strength. The day including firing on the ranges at BEUVRY. Coy billeted at the Battn. all quiet in the line.	R.T.R.
BEUVRY.	2.7.16.		Coy attended Divine Service in the Cinema Hall BEUVRY. at 9 a.m. the remainder of the day spent in finishing preparation to relief.	R.T.R.
BEUVRY.	3.7.16		The Coy relieved 100 M.G. Coy in the CUINCHY SECTOR. Relief completed 11.45 a.m. the Coy manned same 2 Woods Old BOOTS TRENCH Redoubt 16 guns. The Officers and other ranks of the Coy are all quiet in the trenches owing to heavy rain.	R.T.R.
BEUVRY	4.7.16		The Coy in Redoubts carried on with rifle firing on GERMAN Aircraft. Flyover aeroplane etc all quiet in the line. One Other Ranks admitted to enfoncements	R.T.R.
BEUVRY.	5.7.16		Training in Redoubts carried on quiet day in the trenches. 15992 Pte GIBBS.F. struck off the strength & evacuated from Redoubt and 2019 4106 JeLONG wounded by rifle grenade 12.15 a.m. all quiet.	R.T.R.
BEUVRY	6.7.16		Usual hostile inspection all quiet in the line.	R.T.R.
BEUVRY.	7.7.16.		The Coy handed over 1 a.m. & came in evening relieving others alarms and ammunition from the trenches. The Coy relieved by 116 M.G. Coy all quiet.	R.T.R.
BEUVRY & CHOCQUES.	8.7.16		Relief complete 3.30 a.m. The Coy left BEUVRY 4.30 a.m. and marched to CHOCQUES, arriving there 7.30 a.m. billeted in a farm. Transport and HQ 2½ miles off at BETHUNE 1½ miles. The men had and entrained at CHOCQUES Station 11 a.m. arrived at AMIENS 2.20 p.m. 11 hours later followed in various trains marched about ever mile to RAINVILLE 2466 Pte OVERY evaded via RAINVILLE station 2.46 Pte OVERY evaded from Guard Room at CHOCQUES.	R.T.R.
RAINVILLE	9.7.16		The Rear section (D section) reported at RAINVILLE 3 a.m. day billeted in farm Houses and Remainder of day spent in cleaning and refitting from the march Very hot day Walks in the area. No or Bad Accommodation & very difficult first Divisional Boxing tournament	R.T.R.
RAINVILLE	10.7.16		Carried on usual training and refitting and gaining an inspection of guns and rounds were carried out by Sector officer very hot day & end of the day & no casualties	R.T.R.

Army Form C. 2118.

WAR DIARY
or
INTELLIGENCE SUMMARY
(Erase heading not required.)

Instructions regarding War Diaries and Intelligence Summaries are contained in F. S. Regs., Part II. and the Staff Manual respectively. Title Pages will be prepared in manuscript.

Place	Date	Hour	Summary of Events and Information	Remarks and references to Appendices
TRAINVILLE. CORBIE	11.7.16		The Coy paraded at 7.30 a.m. and marched with the brigade to CORBIE all packs were dumped at TRAINVILLE and carried by motor lorries. Packing party sent in advance to allocate billets in Coy area. Officers in CORBIE, the Coy is counted as troops, officers and guns all arrived at the following time. Van Hingh and Pat T. both good.	C.S.S.
CORBIE VILLE-SOUS-CORBIE	12.7.16		The Coy left CORBIE at 2.30 p.m. and marched with brigade to VILLE sour CORBIE there were a 10.20 m routes why covered and dusty, met GERMAN prisoners coming back from the line. The Coy bivouaced in a field, officers had tents, hot air dry also forming of the mine also at 9.00 am. Packs were dumped here before proceeding to the line.	D.S.
VILLE-SOUS-CORBIE MÉAULTE	13.7.16		Today sent on to an premises positions to our front. Country was flat and wooded. The Coy bivouaced at MÉAULTE evening march the GERMAN prisoners and wounded forward down the lanes. De Tochoff old £4.95%	R.S.S.
MÉAULTE FRICOURT	14.7.16		The Coy marched with the brigade and halted on the side of the road in BE CORBEL for several hours, afterwards moved in through FRICOURT to a village W. of this place. Here we camped for the night on side of the hill. Indian cavalry were in attack early in morning.	R.T.S.
MAMETZ WOOD - BAZENTIN LE-PETIT WOOD	15.7.16		The Coy went into action 4 guns being attached to the 10th MIDDLESEX and 4 guns to the 1/4 SUFFOLKS. Came under shell fire Ed MAMETZ WOOD. At attack party sorted a brunt of BAZENTIN-LE-PETIT WOOD. S. of HIGH WOOD and was held up by enemy machine gun fire from vicinity of High wood. Eight guns left in position in S.W. of wood south at S.E. corner of BAZENTIN-LE-PETIT WOOD. Four of these guns were unheard of later up a frontier on ridge S. E. BAZENTIN-LE-GRAND WOOD. Casualties: 1 Officer Lieut. F. E. ALEXANDER wounded in leg, from M.G. (German) O.R. 1 killed, 10 wounded, 1 missing	R.T.S.
BAZENTIN-LE-PETIT WOOD & VILLAGE	16.7.16		Day spent in consolidating positions. Relief of the section out action in remnant. Considerable and odd activity on both sides, many S shells bursting in vicinity of BAZENTIN-LE-GRAND WOOD and rocks be S.W of village. Casualties O.R. 1 died of wounds, 1 wounded.	R.S.S.

WAR DIARY
or
INTELLIGENCE SUMMARY

(Erase heading not required.)

Army Form C. 2118.

Place	Date	Hour	Summary of Events and Information	Remarks and references to Appendices
BAZENTIN-LE PETIT VILLAGE & WOOD	17/7/16		Sections on the E. of BAZENTIN-LE-PETIT VILLAGE relieved by 3 guns of 19th M.G. Coy in the village and CEMETRY. Team guns firing indirect on GERMAN SWITCH TRENCH from position S. of BAZENTIN-LE-GRAND WOOD moved 1800 yds westward still with active rear. Bigfenough around HIGH WOOD GERMAN guns attacked casualties O.R. 2 wounded by rifle fire. Own casualties nil.	S.S & S
BAZENTIN-LE PETIT VILLAGE & WOODS	18/7/16		Section in BAZENTIN-LE-PETIT WOOD shelled throughout the day. Also the wood to the SOUTH suffered a little during relief by men situated in the N. by GERMANS. Casualties O.R. 6 wounded by rifle fire.	S.S & S
BAZENTIN WOODS	19/7/16		Company shelling by our side. German bombarded by our artillery. Its attack on HIGH WOOD and GERMAN TRENCH N. of BAZENTIN-LE-PETIT Barrage fire assisted 2 guns in BAZENTIN-LE-GRAND WOOD delivered 4 guns to relieve L. Coy 6th OB be attached to 2nd Argylls for the attack. Casualties O.R. 1 wounded 2ndLt. [illegible]	S.S & S
BAZENTIN WOODS	20/7/16		At 3 a.m. 56 M.G. Coy came out relieved from guns N. of BAZENTIN-LE-PETIT WOOD team bombarders being carried on by our artillery. 3.25 LI Wilted of HIGH WOOD was carried out and unsuccessful. 2nd ARGYLLS advanced N. of BAZENTIN-LE-PETIT VILLAGE and dug in under cover of darkness. Touch lost between the force and force advancing HIGHWOOD. M.G. uns S. of BAZENTIN-LE-GRAND wood still firing on MARTINPUICH and GERMAN trenches. GERMAN'S C.B. in the day 2 ridges heavily with gas shells and round HIGH WOOD 2 ARGYLLS and 3. 4 M.G. led a lot and the fire Casualties. Officers 2nd Lieut R.E. EVANS. wounded 30.00 fire. 2nd Lieut H.H. BOYNE. Gassed O.R. Wounded 3 gas. 1 shell fire.	S.S & S
BAZENTIN WOODS	21/7/16		Enemy shelling continued again E. of BAZENTIN-LE-GRAND WOOD firing indirect throughout the day at ridge on German lines the N. of BAZENTIN-LE-PETIT VILLAGE and N. of HIGH WOOD at 10. m 57 M.G. Coy relieved A. Coy of all position.	S.S & S

continued

Army Form C. 2118.

WAR DIARY
or
INTELLIGENCE SUMMARY

(Erase heading not required.)

Instructions regarding War Diaries and Intelligence Summaries are contained in F. S. Regs., Part II. and the Staff Manual respectively. Title Pages will be prepared in manuscript.

Place	Date	Hour	Summary of Events and Information	Remarks and references to Appendices
MAMETZ WOOD	21/7/16 cont'd		The Coy. then went back and were in reserve S.E. of MAMETZ WOOD. Teamen occupied and dug shelters. Later it was found heavy shelling causing many casualties. It was decided to move on to SOUTH TOWARDS evening. The enemy sent over many tear shells but their were no serious being to the records of HIGHWOOD and the S.A.A. Casualties O.R. 1 wounded 21.00 Bn. 1 Sergeant	P. R. S.
MAMETZ WOOD	22/7/16		Relieved by 152 M.G. Coy. at 1 am. The Coy. then marched to DERNANCOURT, via FRICOURT, BECORDEL, MEAULTE. Arrived at 6 a.m. at the Coy. went into billets. At 2 pm Coys. and men Roll was arrived from base. Commanding guns in the afternoon. Day's Draft of 30 O.R. arrived	P. R. S.
DERNANCOURT	23/7/16		Coy. Church parade and Rest inspection R.C. Church parade 9 a.m. in village church. Refitting. Rifles and kit inspection. General cleaning up	P. R. S.
DERNANCOURT	24/7/16		Ordinary parade throughout the day. Bearing gun drill and musketry. The G.O.C. inspected the drafts at 10 a.m. Training of the drafts and night firing.	P. R. S.
DERNANCOURT	25/7/16		Training carried on. A news parade. Special orders being had to wait. Briefing special orders read from Major General LANDON comdg. 33rd Div. congratulating the troops on their success in this late enemy bombardment, showing results of gallantry	P. R. S.
DERNANCOURT	26/7/16		The G.O.C. 98th INF BDE Inspected the Contents of 2s Brigade at 10 a.m. The remainder of the Company carried on with usual training. A draft of 170 O.R. arrived from 33 D.A.C. The officers left in charge and would be coming.	P. R. S.
DERNANCOURT	27/7/16		Training carried on. Each Battalion in the Brigade will train enough Machine Gunners to form enough of a course so gun and know their knowledge of M.G. will an N.C.O. of each supplier should be able to go the transfers from the unit.	P. R. S.

2449 Wt. W14957/M90 750,000 1/16 J.B.C. & A. Forms/C.2118/12.

Army Form C. 2118.

WAR DIARY
or
INTELLIGENCE SUMMARY

(Erase heading not required.)

Instructions regarding War Diaries and Intelligence Summaries are contained in F. S. Regs., Part II. and the Staff Manual respectively. Title Pages will be prepared in manuscript.

Place	Date	Hour	Summary of Events and Information	Remarks and references to Appendices
DERNANCOURT	28/7/16		Roman Catholics attended Divine Service at 10 a.m. Instructional class held. Usual parades throughout the day. Work carried on as usual.	R.S.G.
DERNANCOURT	29/7/16		Coy carried out a tactical scheme including Vickers and Lewis Guns. Instructional classes held. Training during the morning. Duties as usual.	R.S.G.
DERNANCOURT	30/7/16		Coy attended Divine Service 10 a.m. Roman Catholics 9.30 a.m. Charge of 17.0.R. refitted from the base. Coy held sports competition. Major General LANDON C.B. G.O.C. 33rd Division distributed the Military Medal Ribbon to those who won it during the recent operations of 3.7.16. 45 per cent of the Coy Officers attended.	R.S.G.
DERNANCOURT	31/7/16		Tactical action on a small field firing carried out by the Coy. the morning. Signalling classes on Wealk carried on.	R.S.G.

S. B. Joy, Capt.
Commanding No. 98 M. G. Coy.

98th Brigade.

33rd Division

98th BRIGADE.

MACHINE GUN COMPANY

AUGUST 1 9 1 6

Army Form C. 2118.

98 M.G. Coy.
Vol 4

WAR DIARY
or
INTELLIGENCE SUMMARY
(Erase heading not required.)

Instructions regarding War Diaries and Intelligence Summaries are contained in F.S. Regs., Part II. and the Staff Manual respectively. Title Pages will be prepared in manuscript.

Place	Date	Hour	Summary of Events and Information	Remarks and references to Appendices
DERNANCOURT	1/8/16		Usual training carried out throughout the day including instruction to the Battalion M.G. class, musketry and field fortifications of DERNANCOURT. Company taking 8 guns to place in the M.G. emplacements. Fired out. Weather very hot and sunny.	2.P.S.
DERNANCOURT	2/8/16		Classes carried on. Company carried out Technical scheme including vickers gun fighting. Battalion M.G. class fired a short course on the range. Weather still very warm.	2.P.S.
DERNANCOURT	3/8/16		Usual instruction given on Lewis & M.G. class on the range. Musketry. 22 day firing of the class. Weather very warm.	2.P.S.
DERNANCOURT	4/8/16		Usual training carried on in the Company. Section fired a Reinforcement range. Rifle of Practices including west fighting of 10% m. Weather dull.	2.S.2.
DERNANCOURT	5/8/16		Usual training carried on. Reconnaissance of line BAZENTIN-LE-GRAND and MAMETZ WOOD. Weather very warm, much dust	2.P.8.
DERNANCOURT & MAMETZ WOOD	6/8/16		Company attended Church Parade at 10 a.m. Transport moved at 12.30 to join B Echelon at BÉCORDEL, marching via MÉAULTE & FRICOURT. Company marched via MÉAULTE. Reached 154 M.G. Coy. Team Pont and shortly Taon to relieve them in MAMETZ WOOD.	2.P.S.
MAMETZ WOOD	7/8/16		Spent evening moving up from rear to advance positions in MAMETZ WOOD. Consolidated our positions were very warm. Then the day was very warm.	2.P.S.
MAMETZ WOOD	8/8/16		Clearing out trenches, getting positions. Information during the day. Casualties. O.R. 1 wounded. Rifle Grenades observed and bombers. Weather warm.	2.P.S.

WAR DIARY
or
INTELLIGENCE SUMMARY
(Erase heading not required.)

98 M.G. Coy

Instructions regarding War Diaries and Intelligence Summaries are contained in F.S. Regs., Part II. and the Staff Manual respectively. Title Pages will be prepared in manuscript.

Place	Date	Hour	Summary of Events and Information	Remarks and references to Appendices
MAMETZ WOOD	9/8/16		Quiet day. Employed carriers on making dug out bombproof &c.	S.P.S.
MAMETZ WOOD	10/8/16		Intermittent shelling by enemy artillery chiefly on east side of MAMETZ WOOD. FINE. Casualties NIL	S.P.S.
MAMETZ WOOD	11/8/16		Reconnoitred trenches in the neighbourhood of HIGH WOOD at 6 a.m. Saw O.R. 100 M.G. Coy & returned to breakfast at 9 a.m. Hard shelling enemy arty on BAZENTIN valley. Fine.	S.P.S.
MAMETZ WOOD	12/8/16		Sections officers reconnoitred the line and BAZENTIN-LE-GRAND VILLAGE casualties O.R. 1 killed 2 Lieut SHERRIFF T.D. returned to join Company from the Base. Bankers Artillery active.	S.P.S.
MAMETZ WOOD & HIGH WOOD	13/8/16		Relieved 100 M.G. Coy at 2.30 a.m. Relief complete at 7 a.m. Took guns in Trenches at HIGH WOOD. Saw guns in BAZENTIN-LE-GRAND VILLAGE. Guns in reserve Officers with R.E.D. Company east of & reconnoitre the line. Casualties 1 O.R. Killed. Howd & Lt. Co. Bn. 6600 rounds fired. Barrage at the edge of enemy trenches between HIGH WOOD and DELVILLE WOOD also MARTINPUICH	S.P.S.
HIGH WOOD	14/8/16		Situation normal. Trenches deepened by M.G. and improvements in emplacements of HIGH WOOD & New emplacement dug in BAZENTIN-LE-GRAND VILLAGE 4000 rounds fired. Barrages on enemy trenches on wife, on Junction dangle. In Prior Line 5.20 p.m. fire opened on a small truck & cannon at E. corner of HIGH WOOD. Casualties O.R. 1 wounded.	S.P.S.
HIGH WOOD	15/8/16		Situation normal. Sudden activity. 700 rounds fired at front BAZENTIN-LE-GRAND village on enemy Barrage. Casualties NIL.	S.P.S.

2449 Wt. W14957/M90 750,000 1/16 J.B.C. & A. Forms/C.2118/12.

WAR DIARY or INTELLIGENCE SUMMARY

Army Form C. 2118.

98 M. G. Coy

Instructions regarding War Diaries and Intelligence Summaries are contained in F. S. Regs., Part II. and the Staff Manual respectively. Title Pages will be prepared in manuscript.

(Erase heading not required.)

Place	Date	Hour	Summary of Events and Information	Remarks and references to Appendices
HIGH WOOD	17/8/16		Heavy artillery duties went on towards evening of 17th. enemy put over a number of tear shell ammunition about S. corner of HIGH WOOD. Officers and men will to know of S.A.A. protectors to attack. Entire remainder informed 7500 rounds SAA distributed	2 D.S.
HIGH WOOD	18/8/16		Whistle artillery again in support and communication trenches. Increased will all night firing. Casualties O.R. 6 wounded. About 20,000 fire 2000 rounds from Coy. 2nd Lt BAZENTIN-LE-GRAND VILLAGE at noon ranged O.C. 19 M.G. Coy came to N Road runs about 212 from m. NE BAZENTIN-LE-GRAND VILLAGE	2 D.S.
HIGH WOOD	19/8/16		Weather fine HIGH WOOD and HIGH WOOD LANE carried out at 2.45. preceded by artillery bombardment, enemy land only slightly damaged. Strong from NE corner of HIGH WOOD solidified from German gun. Battn went to advance as 1 Coy. of Suffolks & E of HIGH WOOD deemed their objective. Return forest to retain the remainder of 1 Coy & ARGYLLS advanced through to HIGH WOOD but also forced to retire. Two machine guns who attacked to head balloon in position hit roll. one no longer knocked and standing. Casualties O.R. 3 killed 6 wounded 3 missing	2 D.S.
HIGHWOOD & FRICOURT	19/8/16		Quick throughout 20 was relieved by 19 M. G. Coy in morning at 5 a.m. Coy is at Camme dug outs & vacated to FRICOURT arrived 5 p.m. bivouacs to remainder of day	2 D.S.
FRICOURT	20/8/16		Cleaning out and refitting of guns from flower etc. 2nd Lieut RENNIE W.K. was & Retired Casualties O.R. 2 wounded accidental gunshot wound. inflicted by enemy's I.O.R. & Registered dry cordum	2 D.S.

WAR DIARY or INTELLIGENCE SUMMARY

Army Form C. 2118.

98 M.G. Coy.

Instructions regarding War Diaries and Intelligence Summaries are contained in F.S. Regs., Part II. and the Staff Manual respectively. Title pages will be prepared in manuscript.

(Erase heading not required.)

Place	Date	Hour	Summary of Events and Information	Remarks and references to Appendices
FRICOURT	21/8/16		Usual in/actions and training carried on the aeroplanes the day. During the morning a number of German aeroplanes came over the lines and dropped bombs, very little damage was done. Very warm.	C.T.S.
FRICOURT BECORDEL	22/8/16		The Coy moved down to Transfers lines during the morning. The 4 men guns of the establishment of the Coy were despatched to Sir Rose bracketing from ALBERT drawn. Two O.R. accidentally wounded by German rifle grenade. Drivers gone ahead unloading the day.	C.T.S.
BECORDEL	23/8/16		Usual parades and carrying out of training. Two guns are now emplaced in front of Trench Schiller during the afternoon & continuously harassing enemy working parties during the night.	S.F.S
BECORDEL	24/8/16		Coy carried out training in the company lines. Addition in the Brigade had an alarm in the middle of the Coy turned out fully equipped in about 25 mins off, 15 minutes after alarm.	S.F.S
BECORDEL	25/8/16		Usual parades in the morning. Capt. Sam proceeded to the school on right of DERNANCOURT WOOD to select 100 M.G. Coy. Recruits contacts 4.30 pm while combats 7.30 a.m. 26" inst.	S.F.S
TRENCHES	26/8/16		Heavy rain all day in the morning the morning 10.R. Killed by stray shot on our fire line. The engine gives 8000 rounds fixed indirect fire on BAZENTIN & LE GRAND on German reserve and 2nd ground behind it.	S.F.S
TRENCHES	27/8/16		Enemy artillery active all over the line. Our Carriers 40 R wounded by enemy shell. our infantry fired 6000 rounds shell indirect on roads leading to 26th inst. 2/Lieut RENNIE wounded from Rapped.	S.F.S
TRENCHES	28/8/16		Had a fair day 26 officers attended down and Recommon Tenders to a very fair and Combatie W.a. Indicates the aeroplanes the night or annual loads.	S.F.S

WAR DIARY
or
INTELLIGENCE SUMMARY

(Erase heading not required.)

Army Form C. 2118.

98 M.G.C. ──────

Instructions regarding War Diaries and Intelligence Summaries are contained in F. S. Regs., Part II. and the Staff Manual respectively. Title Pages will be prepared in manuscript.

Place	Date	Hour	Summary of Events and Information	Remarks and references to Appendices
TRENCHES	29/8/16		2nd Lieut SYMONS E.C. wounded. Relief by officer taking to German line 4000 rounds fired from SAVOY TRENCH on enemy barrage.	E.S.&
TRENCHES	30/8/16		Weather fine. 73 M.G. Coy. moved to relieve 98 Coy at 2.30 p.m. Heavy shelling and incoming fire at 6.30 p.m. Front line. 6.30 p.m. 2 guns attacked 2.30 a.m. & 6 guns in front line 8 a.m. Got into position 2.30 a.m. & 3.15 a.m.	R.F.&
TRENCHES DERNANCOURT	31/8/16		Coy relief capts 3 p.m. Day army units Brigade on Brig. camp. officers went to DERNANCOURT relief by 73 Coy. Weather fine.	R.S.&

E.S. ffry Capt
O.C. 98 M.G.C.

98th Brigade.

33rd Division.

98th BRIGADE MACHINE GUN COMPANY

SEPTEMBER 1 9 1 6

WAR DIARY or INTELLIGENCE SUMMARY

Army Form C. 2118.

(Erase heading not required.)

Vol 5

[Stamp: No. 98 MACHINE GUN COY. 2.10.16 MACHINE GUN CORPS]

Place	Date	Hour	Summary of Events and Information	Remarks and references to Appendices
DERNANCOURT & ALLONVILLE	1/9/16		The Coy. bivouacked out on R.00 N.W. of DERNANCOURT. Day spent in cleaning & gun and equipment. Transport moved off 10.30 to proceed to ALLONVILLE. The remainder of the Coy moved by motor bus at 7 p.m. to ALLONVILLE reaching there destination at 9 p.m. Good billets. Very warm.	R.T.O.
ALLONVILLE FIENVILLERS	2/9/16		The Company moved off at 1.7 a.m. having been on billeting party. ROUTE :- ALLONVILLE, COISY, VILLERS-BOCAGE, PALMAS, LA VICOGNE, VERT-GALAND FM. CANDAS, FIENVILLERS. Reached destination at 5.15 p.m. TB. 22,000 in frames not drawn. Warm & sunny. No of men fell out on the march. O.R. 10.	R.T.O.
FIENVILLERS	3/9/16		Remained in FIENVILLERS. The Company washed and general clean up. Horses & wounds during the day. The Company attended Divine Service at 7 p.m. Subject addressing officiating today was Field one. Strange, 2/Lieut BRICKELL F.W. referred from base depot.	R.T.O.
FIENVILLERS to MEZEROLLES	4/9/16		The Company moved off at 1.7 a.m. arriving back in MEZEROLLES. ROUTE FIENVILLERS, MONTPLAISIR, OUTREBOIS, MEZEROLLES. Reached destination 3.15 p.m. Company 1000 ds in Bourn. Transport in waterfall & civil by servants horses ? No. of men fell out on march O.R. 2. On other ranks admitted to Amplois at DOULLENS. Packs carried on Bourn by the maids.	R.T.O.
MEZEROLLES	5/9/16		The Company moved off at 11.0 a.m. having one on billeting party for HAUTE COTE. ROUTE MEZEROLLES, RENAISNIL, BONNIERES, FORTEL, VACQUERIE, LIGNY, HAUTE COTE. Reached destination 3.30 p.m. The Company billeted in farms, washing but very good billets. Transport in waterfall. Two O.R. admitted to amplois a draft of 6 O.R. referred from Base depot. Two O.R. (namely -------) ------- to ------- ------- Coy. A.S.C.	R.C.S.
HAUTE COTE	6/9/16		The Company remained in HAUTE COTE. Morning spent in cleaning guns and refilling.	R.T.O.

WAR DIARY or INTELLIGENCE SUMMARY

Army Form C. 2118.

Place	Date	Hour	Summary of Events and Information	Remarks and references to Appendices
HAUTE-COTE	7.9.16		The Company still remained in HAUTE-COTE. Ordinary training carried on. The G.O.C visited the Company doing gun drill. He spoke highly of the Company guard on its turning out. Weather fine, the excellent afternoons afforded for sports were made use of.	
HAUTE-COTE & WARLUZEL	8.9.16		The Company moved off at 8.30 a.m. having sent the usual billeting parties ahead. Route – NUNCQ – FREVENT – REBREUVIETTE – BEAUDRICOURT – SUS-ST-LEGER to WARLUZEL. The Company arrived at WARLUZEL at 1.45 p.m. Billets were very bad and crowded. On application to Brigade we were told to move in the morning. Weather fine.	
WARLUZEL & SUS-ST-LEGER	9.9.16		G.O.C held a conference of C os with reference to taking over part of the line. A billeting party forwarded to SUS early, and the Company moved to fresh billets there in the later part of the morning, arriving 1.0 p.m. The cooks were sent on early to avoid the difficulty of getting hot dinners. Weather continues fine.	
SUS-ST-LEGER & GAULTY	10.9.16		The Company moved off early, starting at 9 D a.m. Route WARLUZEL. E end of COULLEMONT. by a country track to LES ANNELLES FERME arriving 9.30 a.m. Billets very good. Day spent in settling in. Weather continues fine. Good drilling ground. 1 R.E hut.	
GAULTY	11.9.16		The Company availed themselves of the fine weather to thoroughly cleaning all Equipment. Guns &c. Opportunity was again taken to devote the afternoon to sport.	
GAULTY	12.9.16		Inspection by O.C. Otherwise ordinary training. A canteen was started in an experiment, and answered very well. 2nd Lieut HARGRAVE reported for duty. One officer and 5 O.R. left for the 3rd Army Rest Camp at BOULOGNE. The Company paraded Church Parade in the evening.	

WAR DIARY or **INTELLIGENCE SUMMARY**

Army Form C. 2118.

Place	Date	Hour	Summary of Events and Information	Remarks and references to Appendices
SAULTY and HUMBERCAMP	13.9.16		The morning was spent in cleaning up and packing. Having rest on the usual billeting party the Coy moved off at 4.15 p.m. Route COUTURELLE - GAUDIEMPRÉ - to HUMBERCAMP, arriving 6.30. Billets bad & leaky. Weather inclined to break.	
HUMBERCAMP	14.9.16		Ordinary parades carried on with. Weather bad. The roads softened considerably from it. The Transport is in a large field about ¼m from the Company. Rent opened again.	
HUMBERCAMP	15.9.16		Ordinary training carried on with. Parties told off to work on building huts, draining the roads, and excavating chalk for Transport standings for the winter. O.C. proceeded on leave. Written letter.	
HUMBERCAMP	16.9.16		Usual training continued. The same fatigue parties were provided. The Weather broke again & there was a good deal of rain.	
HUMBERCAMP	17.9.16		O.C. proceeded to trenches in front of HANNES-CAMP to take over for 19th Contr. aux. Excellent trenches. Usual training continued. Church parade in the morning on Transport ground. G.O.C. again spoke highly of the Company. Band 1.O.R. proceeded on leave.	
HUMBERCAMP	18.9.16		Section officers proceeded early to trenches to look over new position. Weather very bad. 1 Off. 5 O.R. arrived back from no 1 cart at BOULOGNE. 2 O.R. proceeded there. Usual training in the morning. Parties looked over the Orders for trenches. Tomorrow cancelled late at night. A shoemaker was sent to the Coy. by the KINGS.	
HUMBERCAMP & BAVENCOURT.	19.9.16		Y.O.C. & Section Officers proceeded by motor lorry to take over new line in front of HEBUTERNE Trenches from 10th Bn. Seaforth Wraiths & Coy only. In the afternoon the Coy moved off at 2.40 p.m. Route. ST AMAND - SOUASTRE - BAVENCOURT arriving there 4.30 p.m. Transport about a mile & half away near COIGNEUX on very bad ground. Rations did not arrive till 11.30 p.m.	

WAR DIARY or INTELLIGENCE SUMMARY

Army Form C. 2118.

Place	Date	Hour	Summary of Events and Information	Remarks and references to Appendices
BAYENCOURT Trenches	20.9.16		The Company paid out. Moving off at 9.30 a.m. Sections at 10 mins interval the Company proceeded to HEBUTERNE via SAILLY-AU-BOIS to relieve 151st Company. 1 Section remained at BAYENCOURT in Reserve. Transport did movement. Relief complete by noon. 5 guns in Support line, 4 in Reserve line, Bn HEBUTERNE at Sect 2 as Indirect Fire. Very quiet in the line. Weather fair.	J.C.P.
Trenches	21.9.16		Very quiet in the line. Indirect fire carried out on roads behind the German lines. The Reserve Section moved to good billets in SAILLY-AU-BOIS. The Transport remained in COIGNEUX and the Q.M. Stores at BAYENCOURT. A Canteen was opened under Gun. in HEBUTERNE. Very much appreciated by all ranks. Weather fair.	J.C.P.
Trenches	22.9.16		Still very quiet. Work carried out on building new Emplacements so that was handed over was useless when called upon. Indirect Fire carried out by 2 guns on roads behind German lines. Weather good. Indirect fire carried out by 2 guns on roads drying up.	J.C.P.
Trenches	23.9.16		Still very quiet. Work continued on new Emplacements. Heavy indirect fire on German roads where movement has been reported & on various targets. Weather good. Canteen Demands on Canteen kept all possible supply. by 4 guns. I.O.R. proceeded on leave.	J.C.P.
Trenches	24.9.16		2nd in Cd. stalked a little during the day. Probably due to smoke from horn. Work indirect fire continued. Skylights alternating made in allotting M.G. lines to Sections to render cross control easier. Weather good. O.C returns from leave	J.C.P.
Trenches	25.9.16		Enemy artillery slightly active. Chiefly searching for guns. O.C. came to look round the line in direction of Transport to the standing they had been unloading on in the afternoon. I.O.R. returned from rest camp at BOULOGNE. 2 forwarded stores. Indirect fire was carried on	J.C.P.
Trenches	26.9.16		All quiet in the line. A Section relieved by No 3 Section in the line. A Section in reserve in SAILLY-AU-BOIS. Indirect fire and on emplacements carried on. Weather fine & sunny.	J.C.P.

Army Form C.2118.

WAR DIARY
or
INTELLIGENCE SUMMARY
(Erase heading not required.)

Instructions regarding War Diaries and Intelligence Summaries are contained in F. S. Regs., Part II. and the Staff Manual respectively. Title Pages will be prepared in manuscript.

Place	Date	Hour	Summary of Events and Information	Remarks and references to Appendices
T.27.d.T.13.d. Trenches	27/9/16		Enemy trench mortars active, otherwise all quiet. One shell fell in front of 2nd Quarry West at 7.30 p.m. no damage done. Indirect fire 5,500 rounds fired at enemy positions behind enemy front line. Weather a/c good day and night on main roads.	R. S. B.
Trenches	28/9/16		All quiet in the line. The O.O.C. 93rd Inf. Bde. came up to look round HEBUTERNE KEEP and preferred new M.G. emplacements. One morning firing to harass Rother. Indirect fire 9000 rounds fired on enemy lines.	R. S. B.
Trenches	29/9/16		New emplacements started in KEEP amounts of enemy convoys detected the new section. All quiet in the line except for slight enemy airplane activity during the afternoon. Indirect fire on enemy tonight, 9500 rounds fired M.G. fire from enemy in HEBUTERNE during the evening.	R. S. B.
Trenches	30/9/16		All quiet in the line except all morning the day usual carried on in trenches. Indirect firing and emplacement work.	R. S. B.

98th Brigade.

33rd Division.

98th BRIGADE MACHINE GUN COMPANY

OCTOBER 1 9 1 6

Army Form C. 2118.

Vol 6

WAR DIARY
or
INTELLIGENCE SUMMARY
(Erase heading not required.)

Place	Date	Hour	Summary of Events and Information	Remarks and references to Appendices
Trenches at HEBUTERNE	1.10.16		Day quiet. Work on new emplacements in HEBUTERNE KEEP proceeded with Reserve section packed & cleaned limbers. Officers of 143 Coy inspected trenches preparatory to taking over. Billeting party proceeded to SUS ST LEGER	Q.D.S.
SUS-ST-LEGER	2.10.16		Coy relieved by 143 M.G.Coy. Relief commenced at 9.20 a.m. Arrived at billets 2.30 p.m. Day out. Billets good. 1.O.R. rejoined from Rest Camp at BOULOGNE	Q.D.S.
SUS-ST-LEGER	3.10.16		Cleaning clothing and limbers in the morning. Return of incidents from Sections. In the afternoon lecture on open fighting. Promotion. 2nd LT. HEDGELAND to be temp. LT. (dated July 5th)	Q.D.S.
SUS-ST-LEGER	4.10.16		Usual training in the morning. Lecture by Section officers in the afternoon. Subjects for spare parts made out. N.C.O's class at 5 p.m. as usual.	Q.D.S.
SUS-ST-LEGER	5.10.16		Arms drill, physical training, mechanism & stoppages. Cpl FRERE proceeded on leave to United Kingdom. Likewise 1 O.R.	Q.D.S.
SUS-ST-LEGER	6.10.16		Arms drill before breakfast. In the morning a tactical scheme - holding an outpost line - on Brigade manoeuvre area. Cleaning guns in the afternoon with the object of forming a Company band 6 men commenced instruction on drum and fife.	Q.D.S.

Army Form C. 2118.

WAR DIARY
or
INTELLIGENCE SUMMARY

(Erase heading not required.)

Instructions regarding War Diaries and Intelligence Summaries are contained in F. S. Regs., Part II. and the Staff Manual respectively. Title Pages will be prepared in manuscript.

Place	Date	Hour	Summary of Events and Information	Remarks and references to Appendices
SUS-ST-LEGER	7.10.16		Usual training proceeded with Company gun drill included a section competition. Inspection by O.C. In the afternoon inter-section football matches were played	D.S.P.
SUS-ST-LEGER	8.10.16		Baths were at disposal of company from 7a.m. till 12p.m. Voluntary church parade. 1 O.R. evacuated from hospital. Clothing changed at baths	D.S.P.
SUS-ST-LEGER	9.10.16		Arms drill before breakfast. In the morning a tactical scheme. In the afternoon physical drill	D.S.P.
SUS-ST-LEGER	10.10.16		Company drill at 7a.m. Throughout day usual training and lecture. Lt. HEDGELAND and 2nd Lt. ST.HILL proceeded. 3 O.R. evacuated from hospital. 2.Lt. ATHERTON proceeded on leave to United Kingdom.	D.S.P.
SUS-ST-LEGER	11.10.16		Day wet - consequently day was spent in indoor training on the gun, the inspection of the company by the G.O.C. being postponed.	D.S.P.
SUS-ST-LEGER	12.10.16		Arms drill before breakfast. During the morning the G.O.C. inspected the company & commended the steadiness and smartness of men and transport. In the afternoon football was played	D.S.P.

2449 Wt. W14957/M90 750,000 1/16 J.B.C. & A. Forms/C.2118/12.

Army Form C. 2118.

WAR DIARY
or
INTELLIGENCE SUMMARY

(Erase heading not required.)

Place	Date	Hour	Summary of Events and Information	Remarks and references to Appendices
SUS-ST-LEGER	13.10.16		In the morning route march – distance about 9 miles. During the afternoon instruction was given to N.C.O.s in map reading.	Q.P.S.
SUS-ST-LEGER	14.10.16		Usual training was carried on during the day. In the afternoon advantage was taken of the fine weather to play football.	Q.P.S.
SUS-ST-LEGER	15.10.16		Church parade had to be cancelled owing to the rainy weather.	Q.P.S.
SUS-ST-LEGER	16.10.16		Squad drill before breakfast. In the morning a tactical scheme was carried out. In the afternoon care and cleaning of gun. Strength – 10 O.R. arrived from base; 10 O.R. evacuated from hospital.	Q.P.S.
SUS-ST-LEGER	17.10.16		Company drill at 7 a.m.. In the morning a Route March in full marching order. Company paid.	Q.P.S.
SUS-ST-LEGER	18.10.16		One section fired on temporary range on sunken road N.W. of SUS-ST-LEGER. Remainder were occupied in aerial training and combined gun drill. Billeting party proceeded to DAOURS.	Q.P.S.

WAR DIARY
or
INTELLIGENCE SUMMARY
(Erase heading not required.)

Army Form C. 2118.

Place	Date	Hour	Summary of Events and Information	Remarks and references to Appendices
DAOURS	19.10.16		The company left SUS-ST-LEGER at 1 p.m. in motor-buses and travelled via BOUZENCOURT and AMIENS to DAOURS, arriving at 11 p.m. The men were billeted in barns. I.O.R evacuated from hospital.	2 Lt S.
DAOURS.	20.10.16		Guns and limbers cleaned and men rested. During the night 20/21/16 a German aeroplane dropped a bomb on men's billet, wounding 2.O.R. These went to hospital.	2 Lt S.
MEAULTE	21.10.16		Company paraded at 6.45 a.m. and marched via CORBIE to MEAULTE billeted in tents.	2 Lt S.
MEAULTE	22.10.16		Church parade. Men rested. LT. HEDGELAND reported from leave. I.O.R reinforcement arrived from base.	2 Lt S.
	23.10.16		Company left MEAULTE at 10 a.m. and marched to TRONES WOOD arriving at 3.30 p.m. Transport proceeded to CARNOY. Men occupied dugouts found during night. Strength - 1 officer, 2nd Lt. VESPER admitted to hospital (+1 batman); I.O.R proceeded to base for discharge, I.O.R proceeded on leave; 2nd Lt. ATHERTON reported from leave.	2 Lt S.

Army Form C. 2118.

WAR DIARY
or
INTELLIGENCE SUMMARY
(Erase heading not required.)

Place	Date	Hour	Summary of Events and Information	Remarks and references to Appendices
TRENCHES LES BOEUFS	24.10.16		During the morning the O.C. inspected line held by 12 M.G. Coy. At 3.30 p.m. company moved off to relieve 12 M.G. Coy. Dispositions were as follows — 1 section in THISTLE TRENCH, W of LES BOEUFS, 1 section on WINDMILL ROAD, 2 sections moved on reserve on high ground between GINCHY and LES BOEUFS, the other at GUILLEMONT STATION. The long distance and heavy ground at night time made the relief of the first line difficult. It was complete by 2.30 a.m. 25/10/16.	J.S.L.
TRENCHES LES BOEUFS	25.10.16		Weather fair. Trenches cleared as much as possible. Casualties 1 O.R. killed (shell), 1 O.R. wounded (shell). Lt. FRERE proceeded to England to the Machine Gun School at GRANTHAM.	J.S.L.
TRENCHES LES BOEUFS	26.10.16		Weather rainy. New emplacement built in THISTLE TRENCH. Casualties 1 O.R. wounded (shell)	J.S.L.

Army Form C. 2118.

WAR DIARY
or
INTELLIGENCE SUMMARY
(Erase heading not required.)

Instructions regarding War Diaries and Intelligence Summaries are contained in F. S. Regs., Part II. and the Staff Manual respectively. Title Pages will be prepared in manuscript.

Place	Date	Hour	Summary of Events and Information	Remarks and references to Appendices
TRENCHES LESBOEUFS	27.10.16		Weather fair to rainy. Heavy bombardment on right by our artillery during afternoon. 1 O.R. returned from leave.	Q.S.S.
TRENCHES LESBOEUFS	28.10.16		At 6 a.m. after one hours' bombardment an attack was made by 1st Middlesex and 4th Kings Liverpool on RAINY TRENCH and DEWDROP TRENCH. The attack was successful and over 100 prisoners were captured. Guns in the support trench stood-to during and after the assault. Between 3.30 p.m. and 4.30 p.m. the front line positions were heavily bombarded by enemy artillery. 1 O.R. returned from a course at CAMIERS, 1 O.R. proceeded on leave. During the night the 2 reserve sections relieved the 2 front sections.	Q.S.S.
TRENCHES LESBOEUFS	29.10.16		One gun was established in SPECTRUM TRENCH and two emplacements built.	Q.S.S.
TRENCHES LESBOEUFS	30.10.16		Heavy rain at night. 1 O.R. proceeded on leave; 1 O.R. reinforcement reported from Base.	Q.S.
TRENCHES LESBOEUFS	31.10.16		⋆ Lt A. LOMAX reported for duty.	

Q.D. Tay, Capt.
Commanding No. 98 M. G. Coy.

98th Brigade.

33rd Division.

98th BRIGADE MACHINE GUN COMPANY

NOVEMBER 1 9 1 6

Vol 7

MACHINE GUN
COMPANY.
No. KD 494
Date 3.12.16

To 98th Inf. Bde

Herewith copy of War Diary of this unit from 1st to 30th Nov. 1916 inclusive.

A Thomas Lieut for
Capt.
Commanding No. [illegible] M. G. Coy.

Vol 7

Confidential

War Diary of 98th Company,
Machine Gun Corps,
from the
1st to the 30th November, inclusive.

WAR DIARY
or
INTELLIGENCE SUMMARY.
(Erase heading not required.)

Army Form C. 2118.

Place	Date	Hour	Summary of Events and Information	Remarks and references to Appendices
TRENCHES	1/11/16		Lieut LOMAX A reported for duty Depot & appointed Brand in Charge. Lieut HARTSHORN A.W. reported for duty. 1 O.R.	R.B.S.
TRENCHES	2/11/16		2 Lt GOULD. reported for duty for Base Depot. Company relieved at night by 19 M.G. Cy. Z's Bivouacs relieved at CARNOY huts.	R.B.S.
CARNOY	3/11/16		Cleaning of guns clothing & equipment. Pte F. 1 O.R. Evacuated to Hospital	R.B.S.
CARNOY	4/11/16 N.a.		Moved to SAND PITS Coy at MEAULTE	R.B.S.
MEAULTE	5/11/16		Company pan. Guns, Limbers & Clothing cleaned. 1 O.R. Evacuated to C.C.S. & arriving there 2.30 p.m. 3 O.R. to Base Depot.	R.B.S.
MEAULTE	6/11/16		Inspection of Guns, Belts & Spare parts	R.B.S.
MEAULTE	7/11/16		Heavy rain all day preventing any work.	R.B.S.
MEAULTE	8/11/16 12 noon		Transport moved to DUARES 1 O.R. on leave U.K. Company prepared to move Heavy rain.	R.B.S.

WAR DIARY
or
INTELLIGENCE SUMMARY.

Army Form C. 2118.

Place	Date	Hour	Summary of Events and Information	Remarks and references to Appendices
MEAULTE	9/4/16	9.30	Company paraded in full marching order & proceeded to EDGEHILL Stables where they entrained for LANGPRE at 2 p.m.	A.D.S.
		4.20	Arrived LANGPRE Station & marched to LIMEUX (10 miles) arrived 9 p.m. & were billeted. Lt HEDGELAND Offr Cmdt R.T.O. LANGPRE.	A.D.S.
LIMEUX	10/4/16		The day was spent in cleaning & polishing equipment, rifles clothing &c. Lt RENNIE proceeded on leave to U.K. TRANSPORT arrived 7 p.m.	A.D.S.
LIMEUX	11/4/16	10 a.m	Marching order parade by Company Commander. Ordinary training carried on with	A.D.S.
LIMEUX	12/4/16		Ordinary training carried on. Lt LOMAX on leave to U.K. Church Parades	A.D.S.
LIMEUX	13/4/16		Company paraded by sections for Bath at HUPPY. Unit having Canteen opened at HEGRO.	A.D.S.
LIMEUX	14/4/16	2-4	Company paraded & marched to BELLIFONTEIN for the washing of Limbers training as usual.	A.D.S.
LIMEUX	15/4/16		Training as usual. Lt ATHERTON Offr Jnr Rgo LIMEUX. 1 O.R. reported for duty from A.S.C. and 2 O.R. from. AFTERNOON Football 1 O.R. evacuated to C.C.S.	A.D.S.

WAR DIARY
or
INTELLIGENCE SUMMARY.

Army Form C. 2118.

(Erase heading not required.)

Place	Date	Hour	Summary of Events and Information	Remarks and references to Appendices
LIMEUX	16/4/16		Training Carried on as usual. 1 O.R. reported for Base. 1 O.R. reported for Hospital	Q.B.S.
LIMEUX	17/4/16		Training Carried on as usual.	Q.B.S.
LIMEUX	18/4/16		Training as usual. Afternoon Cross-Country run - all ranks.	Q.B.S.
LIMEUX	19/4/16		Church Parade. all denominations. Coys preparing to take Elim for Brigade tournament.	Q.B.S.
LIMEUX	20/4/16		Training as usual. 1 O.R. Evacuated to Hospital. 1 O.R. to Base. Lt HARTSHORN to U.K. on leave. Lt GOOLD to U.K. on leave.	Q.B.S.
LIMEUX	21/4/16		Training as usual. Armourer Sergt: 4th Kings inspected Rifles of Company. 1 O.R. reported for Hospital.	Q.B.S.
LIMEUX	22/4/16		Company paraded by Sections for Baths at HUPPE. Training Carried on as usual.	Q.B.S.
LIMEUX	28/4/16		Company received Training Carried on as usual. 1 Sgt. 15 O.R. reported to Brigade School for a Course. 2 O.R. reported to 99 Field Amb. for First Aid Course. BRIGADE Boxing Tournament at HUPPE.	Q.B.S.

Army Form C. 2118.

WAR DIARY
or
INTELLIGENCE SUMMARY.
(Erase heading not required.)

Instructions regarding War Diaries and Intelligence Summaries are contained in F.S. Regs., Part II. and the Staff Manual respectively. Title pages will be prepared in manuscript.

Place	Date	Hour	Summary of Events and Information	Remarks and references to Appendices
LIMEUX	24/4/16		Training as usual. Lieut LOMAX reported for duty.	Q.B.S.
LIMEUX	25/4/16		Training as usual. 2 O.R. reported for Corps M.G. School. Lieut RENNIE reported off duty.	Q.B.S.
LIMEUX	26/4/16		Church Parade for all denominations. Medical Parade cancelled. 1 O.R. evacuated to Hospital. 2 O.R. to U.K. on leave. Lt. BRICKELL on leave to U.K. Lt. RENNIE to Camiers for M.G. Course.	Q.B.S.
LIMEUX	27/4/16		Training carried on as usual.	Q.B.S.
LIMEUX	28/4/16		Training carried on as usual. Lt. Col. R.G. CLARKE M.G.C. attached XV Corps visited the Company. 2 Lt. ATHERTON & 1 O.R. evacuated to Hospital. Afternoon football.	Q.B.S.
LIMEUX	29/4/16		Training carried on as usual. C.Q.L. Lt. Duncan	Q.B.S.
LIMEUX	30/4/16		Company inspected by G.O.C. 38th Division. Training carried on as usual during remainder of day. 1 O.R. reported for Div. School of Farriery.	Q.B.S.

98th Brigade.

33rd Division.

98th BRIGADE MACHINE GUN COMPANY

DECEMBER 1 9 1 6

War Diary.

98th Machine Gun Company.

From 1-12-16 — 31-12-16.

WAR DIARY or INTELLIGENCE SUMMARY.

(Erase heading not required.)

Army Form C. 2118.

Place	Date	Hour	Summary of Events and Information	Remarks and references to Appendices
LIMEUX	1.12.16		One section was engaged in firing on the range. The remainder of the company carried on ordinary training. In the afternoon the company football team played & defeated the Divisional Coy Team in the semi-final of the Divisional Cup.	C.S. Hedgeland Lt.
LIMEUX	2.12.16		Training as usual. In the afternoon the O.C. allowed a return.	C.S. Hedgeland Lt.
LIMEUX	3.12.16		Nothing and equipment inspection, gun-drill, mechanism, etc. The football team was defeated in the final of the Divisional Cup by the 222nd Coy R.E. In the evening a church service was held.	C.S. Hedgeland Lt.
LIMEUX	4.12.16		The transport moved off at 10 a.m. and halted for the night at ———. The remainder of the company occupied the day in physical training, arms drill. 16 O.R. returned to company from Brigade Bombing school. 2 Lt. VESPER P.E. evacuated to El. K. was struck off the strength. 1 O.R. evacuated to hospital, was struck off the strength.	C.S. Hedgeland Lt.
LIMEUX - BRAY	5.12.16		The company entrained at PONT REMY station at 3 p.m., detrained at MERICOURT stn. and marched to Billets in BRAY, arriving there at 12.30 p.m. Transport arrived at BRAY at 8 p.m. Strength - 1 O.R. struck off strength.	C.S. Hedgeland Lt.

WAR DIARY or INTELLIGENCE SUMMARY.

Army Form C. 2118.

(Erase heading not required.)

Place	Date	Hour	Summary of Events and Information	Remarks and references to Appendices
BRAY	6.12.16		The company rested; guns were cleaned & ammunition overhauled. Two officers reconnoitred the line RANCOURT-BOUCHAVESNES	Cs Hedgeland Lt.
BRAY & CAMP 107.	7.12.16		The company left BRAY at 4 p.m. and arrived at CAMP 107 at 10 p.m. CAPT. C.O. JAY and 2nd LT. H.N. GOOLD were removed to hospital by Field Ambulance. LT A LOMAX assumed command of company. 2LT S.A HARGRAVE being on second in command.	Cs Hedgeland Lt.
CAMP 107	8.12.16		Section Officers reconnoitred the line previous to taking over.	Cs Hedgeland Lt.
MARICOURT WOOD	9.12.16		Company moved from CAMP 107 to tents in MARICOURT WOOD. 1 O.R struck off the strength.	Cs Hedgeland Lt.
TRENCHES	10.12.16		12 guns went into the line BOUCHAVESNES platoon, where the Brigade took over from the 19 Chasseurs Alpins and the 193rd Regiment d'Infanterie. The relief commenced at 4.15 p.m and was complete for the company by 6.30 a.m. All 12 guns for the night of the 10/11 were in the front line system. Trenches were muddy & in poor condition owing to bad state of weather. 2 O.R struck off strength	Cs Hedgeland En.

WAR DIARY or INTELLIGENCE SUMMARY.

Army Form C. 2118.

Place	Date	Hour	Summary of Events and Information	Remarks and references to Appendices
TRENCHES	11.12.16		4 guns in left sector were relieved by 4 guns of 100 Coy on the night 11/12th. The men from these teams proceeded to join the reserve section at BRANIERE. In the line the old French emplacements were rebuilt.	Cs Hedgeland Lt
TRENCHES	12.12.16		3 guns were withdrawn from the front line and the teams were employed in building emplacements in the reserve line. Another RE supervision. Weather wet.	Cs Hedgeland Lt
TRENCHES	13.12.16		Work on emplacements and dugouts in reserve line carried on. In the line there was little shelling but weather conditions were bad. 2 Lt. R. R. ATHERTON reported back from leave.	Cs Hedgeland Lt
TRENCHES	14.12.16		Inter-company relief was effected on the night 14/15th; the 2 front line sections being relieved by the 2 in reserve.	Cs Hedgeland Lt
TRENCHES	15.12.16		Commenced work on emplacements in intermediate line but found ground too sodden to make much headway.	Cs Hedgeland Lt
TRENCHES	16.12.16		Work on emplacements continued. Casualties 1 O R wounded (shell)	Cs Hedgeland Lt

WAR DIARY
or
INTELLIGENCE SUMMARY.

(Erase heading not required.)

Army Form C. 2118.

Instructions regarding War Diaries and Intelligence Summaries are contained in F.S. Regs., Part II. and the Staff Manual respectively. Title pages will be prepared in manuscript.

Place	Date	Hour	Summary of Events and Information	Remarks and references to Appendices
TRENCHES	17.12.16		Line reconnoitred by officers of 100 M.G. Coy. preparatory to relief. Usual work carried on during day.	Lt. Hedgeland
TRENCHES	18.12.16		The company was relieved by 100 M.G. Coy. Relief commenced at 4.30 p.m and was completed by 11.30 p.m. On relief the company proceeded by motor-lorry from MAUREPAS to CAMP 17, near SUZANNE	Lt. Hedgeland
CAMP 17 TRENCHES	19.12.16		The company rested; guns were cleaned. LT J.R. OCKENDON reported for duty from M.G. Base Depot. 1 O.R. struck off strength.	Lt. Hedgeland
CAMP 17	20.12.16		The day was spent in cleaning up. 2LT S.A. HARGRAVE proceeded on leave to U.K. LT C.S. HEDGELAND appointed 2nd in command.	Lt. Hedgeland
CAMP 17	21.12.16		The G.O.C. Division visited the company and presented the military medal to 24791 Sergt. BEARD. L.	Lt. Hedgeland

Army Form C. 2118.

WAR DIARY
or
INTELLIGENCE SUMMARY.
(Erase heading not required.)

Instructions regarding War Diaries and Intelligence Summaries are contained in F. S. Regs., Part II. and the Staff Manual respectively. Title pages will be prepared in manuscript.

Place	Date	Hour	Summary of Events and Information	Remarks and references to Appendices
CAMP 17	22.12.16		Guns, etc, cleaned in preparation for trench tour. On the night of the 22/23rd this company relieved 19 M.G. Coy in the RANCOURT section. 11 guns proceeded to the line, 3 teams in the front line and 8 in the reserve line (only 5 emplacements were handed over in the reserve line). 1 O.R. struck off strength.	Lt Sedgeley
TRENCHES	23.12.16		Work commenced on 2 emplacements in reserve line, one of these was destroyed by shell fire after 3 hours work. Aircraft busy.	Lt Sedgeley
TRENCHES	24.12.16		One section in reserve line relieved section in front line with 3 guns. Emplacements in front line were constantly falling owing to rain and had to be rebuilt. Another emplacement commenced in reserve line. Our artillery active.	Lt Sedgeley
TRENCHES	25.12.16		Lt. HARTSHORN and 20 O.R. proceeded to CAMIERS for a course of instruction at the Machine Gun School. 2 guns from CAMP 21 went to the line to form an anti-aircraft battery. Artillery active in the morning.	Lt Hartshorn

Army Form C. 2118.

WAR DIARY
or
INTELLIGENCE SUMMARY.
(Erase heading not required.)

Place	Date	Hour	Summary of Events and Information	Remarks and references to Appendices
TRENCHES	26.12.16		Front line action was relieved by action in reserve line with 3 guns. Line reconnoitred by officers of 119th M.G. Coy preparatory to taking over.	C.S. Hargreaves
TRENCHES	27.12.16		Hostile aircraft active - 2 guns opened fire on three aeroplanes. On the night of the 27/14/28th the company was relieved by 119 M.G. Company. The relief commenced at 4.30 p.m. and was complete by 9 p.m. After relief the company proceeded by motor lorry to CAMP 112, near BRAY. 2nd Lt. T.D. SHERRIFF reported from leave.	C.S. Hargreaves
CAMP 112	28.12.16		The company rested. One officer and a small billeting party proceeded to VAUCHELLES-LES-DOMART. 3 O.R. struck off strength.	C.S. Hargreaves
CAMP 112	29.12.16		The transport left for ARGOEUVRES at 9.30 a.m. The company marched to EDGE HILL STATION and entrained at 5 p.m. LONGPRE was reached about 9 p.m. The company marched to billets in VAUCHELLES-LES-DOMART arriving before midnight. Billets fair. 10 O.R. reported for duty from M.G. Base.	C.S. Hargreaves

WAR DIARY
or
INTELLIGENCE SUMMARY.

Army Form C. 2118.

Place	Date	Hour	Summary of Events and Information	Remarks and references to Appendices
VAUCHELLES LES-DOMART	30.12.16		Inspection of clothing, equipment etc. The transport arrived about 4 p.m.	See Hedgeland.
VAUCHELLES LES DOMART	31.12.16		Gun material overhauled. 2Lt. GOOLD H.N. was evacuated to England. 2Lt. W.K. RENNIE and 2Lt. R.R. ATHERTON to be Lt. with effect from July 6th 1916 (London Gazette, Dec 21st, 1916)	See Hedgeland

Army Form C. 2118.

WAR DIARY
or
INTELLIGENCE SUMMARY.

(Erase heading not required.)

No. 98
MACHINE GUN COMPANY.

No. ....
Date. ....

Vol 9

CONFIDENTIAL

WAR DIARY
of
No. 98 Machine Gun Company
From 1st January 1917 to 31st January 1917

WAR DIARY
or
INTELLIGENCE SUMMARY

Army Form C. 2118.

No. 03 MACHINE GUN COMPANY.

Place	Date 1917 Jan	Hour	Summary of Events and Information	Remarks and references to Appendices
VAUCHELLES lès-DOMART	1		Day was spent cleaning up clothing & equipment. Following were evacuated sick:- 10806 L/Cpl Dawson A, 14852 Pte Akers E, 10858 Pte Calvert C, 42451 Millican J.	AI.
do.	2	3.30 pm	The Co. inspected the Coy by sections in full marching order. Prior to inspection by G.O.C. 98th Bde. following arrived from Base Depot : 44109 Pte Ralph D, 66783 Pte Rodgerson J.	AI.
do.	3	10 am	Inspection by 98th Bde. Commander. Remainder of the day was devoted to sports.	AI.
do.	4	10:30 am	Coy moved to BETTENCOURT-ST-OUEN. G.O.C. 98th 21 Bde. made known that no training was desired in the afternoons, these being preferably devoted to football &c.	AI.
BETTENCOURT ST-OUEN	5		S.A.A. in belts thoroughly overhauled. A cross country run was held in the afternoon.	AI.
do	6		Capt. C D JAY evacuated sick. Lt D. CAMPBELL appointed to command the Coy (from 19th h.R. Coy). 2/Lt. S.A. HARGRAVE appointed to 2nd in command of 19th h.S. Coy vice Lt. D CAMPBELL (XV Corps wire 2/5.1.17) 13458 Sgt. M. Tooley received the D.C.M. (London Gazette 1.1.17)	AI.
do	7		Sunday. No chaplain available for services.	AI.
do.	8		Training proceeded with. Coy was paid at 3.30 pm	AI.

Army Form C. 2118.

No. 98 MACHINE GUN COMPANY.

Name: ....
Date: ....

WAR DIARY
or
INTELLIGENCE SUMMARY.
(Erase heading not required.)

Instructions regarding War Diaries and Intelligence Summaries are contained in F. S. Regs., Part II. and the Staff Manual respectively. Title pages will be prepared in manuscript.

Place	Date	Hour	Summary of Events and Information	Remarks and references to Appendices
BETTENCOURT ST-OUEN	1917 Jan. 9	3.30 pm	Lt. D. CAMPBELL took over command. No. 1655 Pte. Gillespie H. from 19 h. & Coy. was taken on the strength. Cpl. Reeve H. promoted Sergt. from 2.12.16 in the morning.	AL
do.	10		A & B Sect's firing on range. C.D Sect's carried out tactical schemes. Clean clothing obtained for all N.C.O.'s + men. A "dug out" class for 16 N.C.O's + men commenced under R.E. instruction	RE
do.	11	9.45 am 10.15 2 pm	The C.O. inspected the Coy. & dismounted transport. C.&D. Sect's firing on range; A & B Sect's tactical schemes. All rifles were inspected by Armourer Sergt, 4th Kings (L'pool) Regt.	AL
do.	12	9.30 am	Coy. paraded for a tactical exercise round VIGNACOURT Wood. 22849 Pte. Clark S. sick in England struck off the strength from 2/1/17. 2/Lt. S. A. HARGRAVE, 6. 2nd in Command of 19 Inf. Coy., struck off strength from 5.1.17. 26585 Corpl. Looney T. reverts to Pte. at own request	AL
do	13	3pm 3.30	Training proceeded with S.A.A. in belts overhauled. Sanitary work was carried out in the village. The DADOS. 33rd Div inspected all transport vehicles. 70746 Pte. Phillipson A. appointed Coy. Saddler 2.12.16. 22823 A/Cpl Mathews S appointed Coy Accountant 20.12.16. (Coy Orders d/6.1.17.	AL

No. 98 MACHINE GUN COMPANY.

Army Form C. 2118.

WAR DIARY
or
INTELLIGENCE SUMMARY.
(Erase heading not required.)

Instructions regarding War Diaries and Intelligence Summaries are contained in F. S. Regs., Part II. and the Staff Manual respectively. Title pages will be prepared in manuscript.

Place	Date	Hour	Summary of Events and Information	Remarks and references to Appendices
BETTENCOURT St-OUEN	1917 Jan 14	10.30 am	Church parade & medal distribution by the Divisional General. Gy handed with 4th King's Regt. Following were evacuated sick — 32259 Pte Pratt W.F., 34936 Pte Andrews A, 9093 Pte Cooper A following man having proceeded to Island Water Transport Section, R.E., was struck off the strength. — No. 18339 Pte McMillan R. All blankets were fumigated.	A.L.
do.	15	9.30 am	Coy paraded for a route-march. Transport of B. Section left for forward area with transport of 1st Middlesex Regt. Clipping of mules commenced according to orders of A.D.V.S.	A.L.
do.	16		B & D Sections fired on the range. C Sec. carried Hutchison & 2 O.R. sick returns from HQ School. No. 37986 Pte Broadbent J evacuated sick.	A.L.
do.	17		Coy fired on the range. The O.C. & B Sec. personnel left at 8 am entrained at PONT REMY, detrained at EDGEHILL & marched to Camp 111. 36351 Pte Pinkney A.E. evacuated sick. 2/Lieut. Sheriff & billetting party left for forward area. B Sec. passed under orders of 19th Inf. Bde.	A.L.
do.	18	9.30 am	Transport left for forward area, accompanied by 2/Lt Brickell (T.O.) & Lt Hutchison. Morning was occupied by physical training. B Sec isolated thro' measles in Camp 111. Snow fell continuously.	A.L.
do.	19	6.30 am	Coy entrained at LONGPRE at 9 am, detrained at EDGEHILL at 1.45 pm & marched to Camp 13, where the transport arrived by road at 7.30 pm.	A.L.

Army Form C. 2118.

No. 98
MACHINE C ...
COMPA...

No. ....
Date ....

WAR DIARY
or
INTELLIGENCE SUMMARY.
(Erase heading not required.)

Instructions regarding War Diaries and Intelligence Summaries are contained in F. S. Regs., Part II. and the Staff Manual respectively. Title pages will be prepared in manuscript.

Place	1917 Date JAN.	Hour	Summary of Events and Information	Remarks and references to Appendices
CAMP 13	20	11.45 am	"D" Sec. Moved under orders of 19th Inf. Bde. in place of "B" Sec. & went into the trenches with 2nd A. & S. H., relieving No 3 Mitrailleuse Cie. of the French 33rd Brigade.	AL
do.	21		Church Services in the Camp. Lt. HEDGELAND took the Coy. for a short march in the afternoon.	AL
do.	22	11.30 am	Moved into huts at SUZANNE. The C.O. & Lt. ATHERTON reconnoitred new line to be taken over. 31840 Pte. Carter W. reported to Base Depot.	AL
SUZANNE	23	1.30 pm	Left for the trenches. Relieved 10th M.G. Coy in left Bde. Sector S. of BOUCHAVESNES. HQ. at ROAD WOOD (C.25.b.0.7.) Four guns were placed in front line system, two on left & 2 on right subsectors. Six guns in intermediate line & four with an anti-aircraft section under Lt. HARTSHORN at HOWITZER WOOD. "B" Echelon to FRISE BEND (G.5.c)	AL
Trenches	24		"A" Sec. relieved "D" Sec. in the front line & D Sec. returning to HQ.	AL
do.	25		25 men from 4th Suffolk Regt. reported to "B" Echelon to form a section to replace "B" Sec. in isolation, & went to Coy HQ with Lt. RENNIE.	AL
do.	26		No event of importance occurred. The sector was very quiet.	AL
do.	27		Relieved by 100th M.G. Coy. Relief complete 8.40 pm. After relief the Coy marched to CAMP 19 near SUZANNE, the last details arriving about 11.30 pm.	AL

WAR DIARY or INTELLIGENCE SUMMARY.

(Erase heading not required.)

Army Form C. 2118.

No. 98 MACHINE GUN COMPANY.

Place	Date	Hour	Summary of Events and Information	Remarks and references to Appendices
CAMP 19	1917 Jan 28		Clearing up after the trench tour. Coy was paid out at 2.30 p.m. Pte Green H evacuated with trench foot & 3391 Pte Harrison W.D. wounded on 26th evacuated. 37234 Pte Gilbert J & 22849 Pte Clark S. reptd from Base Depot. 36351 Pte Pickney A.B. also reptd from Depot.	AL
do.	29	8.30 p.m.	No. 10412 Sgt Brine T.R. appointed C.Q.M.S. of 48th M.G. Coy. following promotion now made consequently. 19382 L/cpl Moore B. to substantive rank, 70737 Cpl Lad J. true Sgt. Pte Harris (A/cpl) to the Cpl. An enemy aeroplane dropped bombs on the camp. About 20 animals were killed, none of our men touched.	AL
do.	30	2.30 p.m.	Left for trenches & relieved 19th M.G. Coy. in the Right of CLERY sector. Relief complete 8.30 p.m. 15 guns placed in the line. One gun condemned by Ordnance, the team being at "B" Echelon at FRISE.	AL
Trenches	31		Whole front reconnoitred by the C.O. Present dispositions are 2 sections in front on the mainland, one in reserve, and one at OMMIECOURT, across the river SOMME.	AL

Dauphin Lieut
Commanding 98th M.G. Coy.

Army Form C. 2118.

WAR DIARY
or
INTELLIGENCE SUMMARY.
(Erase heading not required.)

Vol 10

CONFIDENTIAL

WAR DIARY
of
No. 98 MACHINE GUN COY.

from 1st Feb. 1917 to 28 Feb. 1917 inclusive.

Army Form C. 2118.

WAR DIARY
or
INTELLIGENCE SUMMARY.
(Erase heading not required.)

Instructions regarding War Diaries and Intelligence Summaries are contained in F.S. Regs., Part II and the Staff Manual respectively. Title pages will be prepared in manuscript.

Place	Date 1917 FEB	Hour	Summary of Events and Information	Remarks and references to Appendices
Tranchee	1		Nothing unusual occurred. Enemy fairly quiet along the Bde front. Front feet continues.	R.L.
do.	2	1.30 pm	In consultation with 11th Field Coy R.E. a scheme of dugouts was commenced with the object of constructing positions in the Intermediate Line. Lieuts Lomax & Hartshorn attended a demonstration by the R.F.C. near Camiers III.	R.L.
do.	3		A Sec relieved A Sec in the front line in left Subsector. Relief complete 10.15 pm.	A.L.
do.	4	10.0 am to 4.14 pm 8.30 am	Lt. Ockenden left for B. Echelon. A bombardment of left Bde. front (100th Bde.) was commenced at 10 am & rose to intense from 4-4 pm. Enemy retaliation fairly lively, mostly with rifle grenades & trench mortars. The O.C. went round the Bde front with the Bde Major.	A.L.
do.	5	10 to 3 pm	Heavy Artillery engaged enemy front line in front of right subsector. Retaliation by shell fire not very heavy; high shrapnel burst over the front line HQ. Lt. Ockenden took over B Sec. from 2/Lt Skerritt, who proceeded to Transport Lines. Hard frost still continues.	R.L.
do.	6	4.30 am	Bombardment, chiefly of left (100th) Bde. front by all calibres. Intense fire from 4.30 pm. to 4.33 pm., during which 4 trench guns co-operated with 20 other m.g's belonging to 100th Bde. & 4th Division, firing rapid (250 rounds per min) ten positions just S. BOUCHAVESNES. Fire slower opened (150 rds. per min) from 4.49 pm to 5 pm. Considerable moral effect on enemy, who brought to bear considerable reinforcements annulled from lung support. Six	A.L.

#3353 Wt. W.2544/1454 700,000 5/15 D.D.&L. A.D.S.S./Forms/C. 2118.

WAR DIARY
or
INTELLIGENCE SUMMARY
(Erase heading not required.)

Army Form C. 2118.

Place	Date 1917 FEB	Hour	Summary of Events and Information	Remarks and references to Appendices
Trenches	7	6:30 pm	A Sec. relieved D Sec. in front line (left) positions, D Sec. occupying positions in reserve vacated by A Sec. Lt. Hantelman took over A Sec. vice Lt. Hedgeland. Transport lines At 11pm 100 Bde. raided enemy trenches opposite them but little or no retaliation fell on our front. C Sec. fired 3500 rounds indirect fire at C.T. 04 paths.	AL
do.	8		Day was quiet + uneventful. Enemy artillery normal; own own rather active. No firing carried out from any position. Hand trot continued. Leave to U.K. opened.	AL
do.	9	3:30 pm	The day was uneventful. Our Heavies were busy in the afternoon. Our anti-aircraft teams fired on enemy aeroplanes over CLERY; but no hits Mand. About 1000 rounds fired at aerial targets. All leave to U.K. suspended.	AL
do.	10	1am 2:30 pm	Our Heavies bombarded the enemy's front line system opposite the left Subsector, firing about 150 rounds. The usual retaliation was made with trench mortar bombs + rifle grenades. At 2:30 pm another bombardment by all calibres opened along the Bde front, slackening off at 6 pm but continuing throughout the night. Lieut. W.B. HORSBURGH reported for duty. B. Section came back from isolation + took over 4 guns in front line. A. Sec. went into reserve + reinforcements arrived at Coy HQ.	AL
do.	11	10:30 am 6:15 am	25 men from 4/ Suffolks who comprised E Sec returned to Cleem unit Bombardment rose to intense + continued till 6:35 am. 8 guns (4 allotted in Intermediate Line near L'Elen Trench 4 at OMNIECOURT) fired barrage onto allotted area near L'Elen Trench 4 at OMNIECOURT) but the bombardment by enemy from 12 noon to 3pm was very great. A further bombardment This comprising — shell fire — shell HORSBURGH took to C Sec. 4 guns than at OMNIECOURT.	AL

WAR DIARY
or
INTELLIGENCE SUMMARY.
(Erase heading not required.)

Army Form C. 2118.

Place	Date 1917 FEB	Hour	Summary of Events and Information	Remarks and references to Appendices
Trenches	12		Intermediate line reconnoitred previous to the placing of 2 guns therein taken at CLERY CHATEAU was cleared for occupation. Received news that 3 horses were killed & 1 wounded last night by bombs dropped from an aeroplane on transport lines at FRISE.	A L
do	13	9.30 p.m.	One gun placed in CLERY CHATEAU (H.12.b.3.8) and one placed in Intermediate line at I.a.O.6. At 9:30 p.m. a Coy of 4th Suffolk Regt. raided enemy trenches on PERLY BULGE. Four prisoners were obtained but were killed by shell-fire before reaching our trenches. We supplied flanking fire with 2 guns. 2000 rounds fired.	A L
do	14		One gun placed in CLERY CHATEAU. Details of relief arranged with OC 100 M.G. Coy. Sgt. SCOTT reported from 20th M.G. Coy. for duty as CQMS.	A L
do	15	3.30 p.m.	Relieved in the line by 100th M.G. Coy. Relief complete 8:30 p.m. All on position were taken over except the 3 guns at Coy HQ, 2 of which were moved to positions in the Intermediate line. Coy marched to Camp 1, SUZANNE.	A L
SUZANNE (Camp 1)	16		The day was spent in cleaning up of clothing & equipment. Coy was paid in the afternoon. Bombs were dropped by German aeroplane near the Camp.	A L
do	17		Guns, belts &c. were overhauled. Gas helmets inspected during the afternoon. Lt. Horsburgh commenced a course of instruction (4 men per one) in mechanism of Coy Lewis Gun at 3.30. 5 p.m. Major E.D. JAY reported from Base Depot & took over command of the Coy.	A L

Army Form C. 2118.

WAR DIARY
or
INTELLIGENCE SUMMARY.
(Erase heading not required.)

Instructions regarding War Diaries and Intelligence Summaries are contained in F.S. Regs., Part II. and the Staff Manual respectively. Title pages will be prepared in manuscript.

Place	Date 1918 Feb	Hour	Summary of Events and Information	Remarks and references to Appendices
SUZANNE (Camp 1)	18	am 9.30	Clothing & kit inspections were held in the morning. The new small box respirators were issued during the afternoon. Coys left for No. 46 Inft Coy on attainment thereto as C.S.M. R.C. Service at SUZANNE Church in the morning.	A.L.
do.	19	3.0 p.m.	Parade in gun drill, physical exercises or from 9.15 am to 3.30 pm. Officers attended a lecture on contact control by O.C. 52nd Sqdn R.F.C.	A.L.
do.	20	pm 2.30	Rain interrupted outdoor parades. Lt. Schenker & 9 N.C.O.'s attended a demonstration by Div. Gas Officer at Camp 18 on the small box respirator. The A.D.V.S., 33rd Divn., inspected transport animals.	A.L.
do.	21		Training carried on indoors throughout the day. No. 23384 L/Cpl. Bradshaw J. promoted corporal.	A.L.
do.	22		New trenches to be taken over were reconnoitred by the O.C. and Lieut. Hedgeland. Training carried on as usual.	A.L.
do.	23	9 a.m.	Coy. moved off to relieve No. 19 M.G. Coy in the BETHUNE ROAD Sector B. Echelon moved to FRISE BEND. Six guns in front line, six in support, four in Intermediate Line (Corps line). All guns relieved in daylight, except two left guns in front line. Relief complete 9.30 p.m. Trenches very wet & muddy. All quiet along the line.	A.L.
Trenches	24		Misty but fine, all standing. All quiet in the line. Some enemy rifle grenades in front line, especially on the left. No casualties	A.L.

Army Form C. 2118.

WAR DIARY
INTELLIGENCE SUMMARY.
(Erase heading not required.)

Place	Date 1917 FEB	Hour	Summary of Events and Information	Remarks and references to Appendices
Trenches	25		Misty. Hostile rifle grenades active along front line trench. At midnight 25/26 2nd A.V.S. Hrs sent over a strong patrol to ascertain the strength of the enemy's front line & if possible to secure a prisoner from HERSFELD TRENCH. Two M.G.s covered flanks of patrol. Hostile trench found to be heavily held. Identification brought back after bombing enemy's front line. Lt. Ockenden +2 OR left, S/Sgt Conrae + H.E. Schor	AL
do.	26		All quiet in the line. 1 OR admitted to hospital with trench-foot. Sections slightly thinned, relieved from trenches for schools.	AL
do.	27		Fine + clear day. Sections in front line relieved by sections in support + intermediate lines, owing to the wet state of dugouts in front line. The 100th Bde (on the right) (WORCESTER Regt) carried out a successful raid during night of 27/28, capturing 22 prisoners (Guard Div.) besides inflicting heavy casualties. Enemy barrage fell on Support + Intermediate lines. Three direct hits on a M.G. dugout in the latter line but no casualties.	AL
do.	28		All quiet. Raid carried out by 2nd A.V.S. Hrs during night of 28/1st but enemy in HERSFELD Trench too strong or prepared for the raid. M.G.'s guarded flanks of raiding party & fired 3000 rounds.	AL

E. S. Gaye, Major
Commanding No. 98 M.G. Coy.

CONFIDENTIAL
Vol XI

War Diary
No 98 Machine Gun Coy.
for
March 1917.

No. 98 MACHINE GUN COY.
31-3-17
MACHINE GUN CORPS.

Army Form C. 2118.

WAR DIARY
or
INTELLIGENCE SUMMARY.
(Erase heading not required.)

Place	Date	Hour	Summary of Events and Information	Remarks and references to Appendices
TRENCHES	MAR 1917 1		All quiet in the line. Sections in front line relieved by those in intermediate & support lines. Relief complete 8 pm.	A2.
do.	2		Enemy's artillery active on left of the sector. No event of any importance occurred. Weather fine throughout the day.	A2.
do.	3		Fine weather continues; artillery active on both sides.	A2.
do.	4	5.15 am	The 8th Div. on our left carried out an attack on German line system. Smoke was discharged opposite on sector. Attack was successful: 150 prisoners & 2 machine guns taken. Gun barrage arranged by XV Corps H.Q. Offrs successful.	A2.
do.	5		Enemy displayed great nervousness, especially on left of sector. The three right-hand positions were handed over to 19th M.G. Coy. Casualties 1 O.R. killed, 1 wounded shell fire.	A2.
do.	6		Snow during the night. All quiet in the line. Took over 3 positions on the night of 25th M.G. Coy. O.C. 120th M.G. Coy reconnoitres the line in the morning.	A2.
do.	7		All quiet throughout the day. The Coy was relieved by 120th M.G. Coy. Relief complete 7.45 pm; Coy proceeded after relief to Camp 1, SUZANNE	A2.

WAR DIARY
or
INTELLIGENCE SUMMARY

Army Form C. 2118.

Place	Date	Hour	Summary of Events and Information	Remarks and references to Appendices
SUZANNE	8		Morning spent in cleaning up. 1.30 pm. moved off. Through BRAY & ETINEHEM and CHIPILLY for SAILLY-LAURETTE, Camp 12, E lines. March complete 4.30 pm. 3 O.R. reinforcements arrived.	A2
SAILLY-LAURETTE	9		Day spent in cleaning up. 4 O.R. reported from Base. 2 Lieut D Campbell transferred to 19th M.G. Coy. 4 O.R. struck off strength of Coy.	RW
do.	10		Washing limbers. 3 O.R. reported from Base. 2 O.R. struck off the strength of Coy. 1 O.R. returned from hospital.	RW
do	11		Parade of G.O.C. Division.	RW
do	12		Bath Parade. Cleaning guns &c. 1 O.R. evacuated to C.C.S.	RW
do	13		Coy sickness in rearguard action. Lt W.R. HORSBURGH temporarily 2nd in command and vice Lt A. O'MAXON hospital.	RW
do	14		Route march.	RW
do	15		Gun drill and musketry.	RW
do	16		Limber cleaning & musketry range. Route march in afternoon. 1 O.R. evacuated to hospital. 1 O.R. arrived from Base depot.	RW
do	17		Divisional entries of M.G. Officers. Coy. cleaning up. 9 O.R. joined from NZ. S. 6 O.R. from Base. (1 O.R. transferred to W.R. HORSBURGH resumed command 2nd /command	RW
do	18		Church Parade in evening. Maj. C.D. JAY on leave. Lt HORSBURGH 2nd /command	RW
do.	19	9.30	Route march. Six reinforcements arrived from Base Depot	A2
	20		Bathing parade. Gun instruction in the afternoon.	A2

Army Form C. 2118.

WAR DIARY
or
INTELLIGENCE SUMMARY.
(Erase heading not required.)

Instructions regarding War Diaries and Intelligence Summaries are contained in F. S. Regs., Part II. and the Staff Manual respectively. Title pages will be prepared in manuscript.

Place	Date 1917 MARCH	Hour	Summary of Events and Information	Remarks and references to Appendices
SAILLY-LAURETTE	21		Range practice & drill parades during the day. Lieut. A LOMAX returned from hospital & took over command.	AL
do.	22		Range practice & drill parades proceeded with.	AL
do.	23		Route march. 1 reinforcement reported from Base Depot. Lieut W.B. HORSBURGH left to take over command of No. 62 M.G. Coy.	AL
do.	24		C.O. inspected billets. Pay parade.	AL
do.	25		Church parade at Camp 12. All blankets disinfected.	AL
do.	26		Indoor training owing to wet weather.	AL
do.	27		Drill parades during the day. Lt. Hutcheon commenced a class on airplane spotting.	AL
do.	28	9.0 a.m. 3 p.m.	Tactical scheme (outpost) in neighbourhood of SAILLY-LE-SEC. The O.R. attended a gas demonstration at Camp 12	AL
do.	29		Gun drill, revolver practice & steady drill parades. 1 O.R. evacuated.	AL
do.	30		Route march S. of river SOMME. Heavy rain all day.	AL
do.	31		Preparations for the move. Major JAY returns from leave & resumed command.	AL

C.D. Jay, Major
Comdg. No. 98 M.G. Coy.

CONFIDENTIAL.

Vol 12

WAR DIARY. of No. 98 Machine Gun Company
from 1st to 30th April 1917.

WAR DIARY
or
INTELLIGENCE SUMMARY.
(Erase heading not required)

Army Form C. 2118.

No. 93 MACHINE GUN COMPANY.

Place	Date	Hour	Summary of Events and Information	Remarks and references to Appendices
SAILLY LAURETTE	APRIL 1917 1	am 9.10	Moved off for BUSSY-les-DAOURS; via WARFUSÉE - ABANCOURT - FOUILLOY - DAOURS. March complete 2 pm. 2 O.R. fell out. Weather changeable.	A.L.
BUSSY-les-DAOURS	2	pm 2.15	Morning occupied in section inspection. At 2.15 moved off for RAINNEVILLE, via QUERRIEU & St GRATIEN. March complete 5 pm. No men fell out. Marched from QUERRIEU to RAINNEVILLE through very heavy snowstorm.	A.L.
RAINNEVILLE	3	11.30 pm	Section inspections in the morning. Moved off for LA VICOGNE, via VILLERS BOCAGE and TALMAS. March complete 4.30 pm. No men fell out. Weather rainy & overcast.	A.L.
LA VICOGNE	4	am 9.30	Moved off for GEZAINCOURT, via BEAUVAL. March complete 1 pm. No men fell out. Weather improving.	A.L.
GEZAINCOURT	5	pm 1.30	Moved off for POMMERA, via DOULLENS, AMPLIER & HALLOY. March complete 4.40 pm. No men fell out. Weather fine & sunny.	A.L.
POMMERA	6		Guns cleaned & limber-wheels greased. Weather still fine. 2 O.R. evacuated sick.	A.L.
do.	7	am 9.30	Moved off for COUIN, via HALLOY, THIEVRES & St LEGER. March complete 1.30 pm. No falling out - NIL. Weather still fine.	A.L.

Instructions regarding War Diaries and Intelligence Summaries are contained in F.S. Regs., Part II. and the Staff Manual respectively. Title pages will be prepared in manuscript.

WAR DIARY
or
INTELLIGENCE SUMMARY.

(Erase heading not required.)

No. 93
MACHINE GUN COMPANY.

Army Form C. 2118.

Place	Date 1917	Hour	Summary of Events and Information	Remarks and references to Appendices
COUIN	April 8	1.30 pm	Moved off for BERLES-au-BOIS, via SOUASTRE, BIENVILLERS. March complete 3.30 pm. No one fell out. Billets moderately good. A German aeroplane was seen flying high at about 4.30 pm.	AL
BERLES-au-BOIS	9	5.30 am	Brigade placed under 6 hours notice to move forward to take part in Third Army operations. Preparations made accordingly. S.D. caps, haversacks & greatcoats dumped. Three days iron ration drawn. Weather very stormy at intervals.	AL
do.	10		Still awaiting operation-orders. SAA in belts cleaned & charged. Very stormy weather; frost during the night.	AL
do.	11		Baths in the morning. At 2 pm warning order to move received. At 7.30 pm moved off via RANSART to BLAIREVILLE, through heavy snow the whole way. At 10.30 pm arrived outside BLAIREVILLE and remained there owing to a traffic-block until about 1.30 am, when the Coy took shelter in a large mined quarry.	AL
BLAIREVILLE	12		Breakfasted about 10 am. The CO went forward at 12 noon to reconnoitre, and at 2 pm moved off via FICHEUX to a reserve line about 1 mile S.W. of MERCATEL, accompanied by the 8 fighting-limbers. B Echelon & the "first reinforcements" remained in BLAIREVILLE.	AL

WAR DIARY

INTELLIGENCE SUMMARY.

Army Form C. 2118.

No. 98 MACHINE GUN COMPANY.

Place	Date 1917	Hour	Summary of Events and Information	Remarks and references to Appendices
Sucker rad in fd SW of MERCATEL	APRIL 13		Bivouacs in. improved. Weather slightly improved. No event of any importance occurred.	AL
do.	14		Bad weather again. "B" Echelon moved to BOISLEUX-au-MONT. Still awaiting movement orders.	AL
do.	15		Fine in the morning, but overcast later. Still under orders to move forward.	AL
do.	16		First reinforcements moved from BLAIREVILLE to join "B" Echelon. At 5 p.m. the Coy together with 8 fighting-limbers, moved off for the trenches via BOIRY-BECQUERELLE and HENIN-en-COJEUL. Relieved 19th M.G. Coy in the line. 4 guns of A Sec. took up position in HINDENBURG line near enemy's block 200 yds. W. of FONTAINE-les-CROISILLES. 4 guns of D Sec. in strong points 1000 yds. W. of this point. 4 guns of B Sec. in HINDENBURG Support line in reserve. 4 guns of C Sec. protecting artillery in rear of this line. Relief complete 11:30 p.m.	AL
Trenches	17		Enemy's artillery active, especially on left of the line. Weather bad & trenches very muddy.	AL
	18		Day spent in bringing up S.A.A. from Bde. dump to Sectional HQ. Heavy shelling 7–9 p.m.	AL
	19		Lieuts. C.S. HEDGELAND & R.R. ATHERTON left for DOULLENS for interview with representative of R.F.C. Lieut. HARTSHORN v. OCKENDEN relieved them. Enemy 2 O.R. evacuated sick	AL

Army Form C. 2118.

WAR DIARY
INTELLIGENCE SUMMARY.
(Erase heading not required.)

No. 98 MACHINE GUN COMPANY.

Instructions regarding War Diaries and Intelligence Summaries are contained in F. S. Regs., Part II. and the Staff Manual respectively. Title pages will be prepared in manuscript.

Place	Date	Hour	Summary of Events and Information	Remarks and references to Appendices
Trenches	APRIL 1917 20		All quiet in the line throughout the day. Weather changed to fine & sunny.	A1
do.	21		New strong point built behind line to protect a battery of artillery placed on our right. 1 M.G. & 1 Lewis gun with a platoon as garrison.	A1
do.	22		During afternoon an artillery carried out a bombardment upon enemy's block on the right of our line. M.G.'s in this part of line were withdrawn to 400 yds this side of the block.	A1
do.	23	am 4:45	The Division attacked the ridge overlooking SENSEE Valley & the HINDENBURG line as far as the 50 contour line S. of the SENSEE. No. 98 M.G. Coy. ordered to cover the consolidation of the final objective with 2 sections. One section was in Bde reserve, & 2 guns of the remaining section covered advance of the tanks; remaining 2 guns occupied strong points protecting on artillery. Final objective in the HINDENBURG line was taken without much opposition, many prisoners being captured. The guns in HINDENBURG line moved up to within 200 yds of final block & protected the flanks of this line. Several large parties were engaged with success by these guns. Later on troops were forced to retire owing to lack of bombs, & the M.G.'s did their best to cover the retirement. 2 guns were knocked out by hostile artillery fire	A1

WAR DIARY
or
INTELLIGENCE SUMMARY.
(Erase heading not required.)

Army Form C. 2118.

No. 93 MACHINE GUN COMPANY.

Place	Date	Hour	Summary of Events and Information	Remarks and references to Appendices
Trenches	APRIL 23 /17		fire & one gun mines the lock had to be abandoned. At this juncture 2 more guns were sent up to the HINDENBURG line to reinforce, at about 10.45 am. The section on left with 2 guns reached German front line & took up positions to protect the left flank. The 2 guns on their right, losing direction, came into HINDENBURG line 1. — did useful work there. No. 8 guns were captured ('87'), as well as many machine guns.	A.
		1pm	After 24 mins bombardment another attack was launched to gain final objective. This however failed. Intermittent hostile bombardment throughout the night. Casualties — 2 OR killed, 4 OR missing, 7 OR wounded.	
do.	24		During the night the Germans had evacuated all ground N of SENSEE river, & our troops pushed forward to occupy this territory. HG's moved forward & took up suitable positions in rear of the front line. Patrols were sent forward into FONTAINE les CROISILLES. Coy was relieved in the trenches by 19 MG Coy on night 24/25. Relief complete 2 am.? Coy then proceeded to bivouacs on HENIN — NEUVILLE - VITASSE road	A.

WAR DIARY
or
INTELLIGENCE SUMMARY.

Army Form C. 2118.

No. 98 MACHINE GUN COMPANY.

Place	Date	Hour	Summary of Events and Information	Remarks and references to Appendices
HENIN-SUR-COJEUL	April 1917 25		Day was spent in resting and cleaning up &c. Some guns were out of action, one missing & 3 rendered useless by shell fire.	AZ
do.	26	10 am	Moved off for BELLACOURT, via BOISLEUX-au-MONT, FICHEUX, BLAIREVILLE and RIVIERE. March complete 2 pm. B & C Sections sent on detachment duty to DAINVILLE and ACHICOURT respectively, for anti-aircraft duties on VII Corps Ammunition Dumps. These guns reported in position about 5 pm 2/Lt C.L. MARSHALL & 8 OR reported for duty.	AZ
BELLACOURT	27		The CO visits B & C Secs. in company with VII Corps M.G.O. Indent Strines from section to complete establishment. Weather continues fine. Cos paid out.	AZ
do.	28		Rifles were examined by armourer. Kit inspection held. Lieut. HEDGELAND left on leave to UK.	AZ
do.	29	10 am	Brigade Church Service attended by VII Corps Commander, after which medals were presented for heavy/swing recent operations.	AZ
do.	30		Training proceeded with. Baths in the afternoon. Linters washed.	AZ

R. B. Gay. Major
Commanding No. 98 M.G. Coy.

No. 98 MACHINE GUN COMPANY.
Date 1.5.17

No 98 MACHINE GUN COY. ✻ MACHINE GUN CORPS.
1-6-17

CONFIDENTIAL

Vol 13

War Diary
of
No. 98 Machine Gun Company
for the
month of May 1917

WAR DIARY
INTELLIGENCE SUMMARY.
(Erase heading not required.)

Army Form C. 2118.

Place	Date	Hour	Summary of Events and Information	Remarks and references to Appendices
BELLACOURT	MAY 1917 1	9 am	A + D Sections moved up to relieve C + B Sections on anti-aircraft duty respectively at ACHICOURT and DAINVILLE. Relief complete about 2 p.m. At 3 p.m. the General held a conference on the recent operations. All the Officers except the T.O. attended.	A2
do.	2	2 pm	Moved off to AYETTE, via RANSART and ADINFER. Reached through very hot weather, had complete 4 p.m. In bivouacs S.E. edge of village. 1 O.R. evacuated sick.	A2
AYETTE	3		Constructed bivouacs in the morning. D Sec moved from DAINVILLE after relief by VI Corps about 3 p.m., + A Sec. from ACHICOURT about 5 p.m.	A2
do.	4		Cleaned + changed all S.A.A. in belts. 4 new guns arrived and taken over by A. + D. Secs.	A2
do.	5		New guns tested on a small range near bivouacs. Training carried on during the day.	A2
do.	6	10 am	Church parade with 98th Trench Mortar Batt. 4 guns mounted to guard a Bde Gymkhana from aeroplane attacks. Dismounted at 7.30 p.m.	A2
do.	7		Divisional Gymkhana at 2.30 pm. 4 guns mounted for anti aircraft purposes. Very hot all day.	A2

WAR DIARY or INTELLIGENCE SUMMARY.

(Erase heading not required.)

Army Form C. 2118.

Place	Date	Hour	Summary of Events and Information	Remarks and references to Appendices
NETTE	MAY 1917 8		Heavy rain throughout the day. Evening spent in improving bivouacs.	AL
do.	9		Fine morning, clearing towards noon. At 10 am all officers attended a M.G. conference, at which the Div. G. Staff, all Brigadiers, C.O's & M.G. companies attended. In the afternoon Coy. sports were held. No parades evening	AL
do.	10		Morning spent in training. Very hot throughout the day.	AL
do.	11	1:30 pm	Moved off for HENIN via BOISLEUX-au-mont. Arrived HENIN about 4 pm & took over positions in the HINDENBURG line opposite FONTAINE- leg-CROISILLES. 4 guns only in position, remainder in reserve at Coy. HQ "B" Echelon at BOYELLES.	AL
Trenches opp. FONTAINE	12		Major JAY went sick and went out of the line. Leut LOMAX took over command. 4 gun positions in our Bde area were taken over by Neighbour Bde. Relief complete about 12 midnight. Their reported from leave	AL
do.	13		One position & taken over in error from 100th Bde, was vacated, & the gun withdrawn to a position in the reserve line, running from the HINDENBURG line to the HENIN-CROISILLES road.	AL
do.	14		A gun was placed in position on the cross roads formed by the roads HENINEL-CROISILLES and HENIN-FONTAINE, firing down the valley in a South-easterly direction. 9 guns now in position. 7 in reserve.	AL

WAR DIARY

INTELLIGENCE SUMMARY.

(Erase heading not required.)

Army Form C. 2118.

Instructions regarding War Diaries and Intelligence Summaries are contained in F. S. Regs., Part II. and the Staff Manual respectively. Title pages will be prepared in manuscript.

Place	Date	Hour	Summary of Events and Information	Remarks and references to Appendices
Trenches opposite FONTAINE	MAY 1917 15		Conveyance on Bde. HQ. moving to a point between HENIN and BOYELLES. Coy. HQ. moved there also. The C.O. reconnoitred the 18th Div. front with a view to selecting positions for barrage fire. Sgt. Lord, J.X. left for Chinese Labour Batt.	AL
do.	16		A concrete position in the HINDENBURG Line occupied by 2 guns firing on to FONTAINE village. Operations for 17th postponed 3 days. Wet in the evening.	AL
do.	17		C. Sec. relieved by A Sec. in front line & B Sec. relieved by D Sec. in reserve. Relief complete about 6 p.m.	AL
do.	18		Belt boxes brought up in the evening for the overhead barrage for operations on 20th. Artillery active on both sides.	AL
do.	19		Lt. Hodgeland departed for a course at CAMIERS. B & C Secs. brought up to positions on left Div. front preparatory to the attack.	AL
do.	20	AM 5.15	The Division attacked the HINDENBURG line between Trenches and the HUMP. 98th Bde. attached) along the SENSEE river bed, but after severe fighting did not make any great progress. One gun was advanced to a position near our original block. At 7.30 p.m. the attack was renewed, with a further short advance as the result. One gun placed on either side of HINDENBURG system along RIVER ROAD, & position was then consolidated. B & C Secs. provided for both attacks.	AL

WAR DIARY
INTELLIGENCE SUMMARY
(Erase heading not required.)

Army Form C. 2118.

Place	Date	Hour	Summary of Events and Information	Remarks and references to Appendices
Trenches oft FONTAINE	MAY 1917 20 ctd.		an indirect barrage about 500 yds in length at ranges of 2300 to 2800 yds., falling on the S.E. edge of FONTAINE village. Our casualties during the whole fighting were nil. Major CD JAY evacuated to 44 C.C.S. & 1 O.R. went on leave.	AL
do	21		The day was quiet except for occasional shelling. The ground on the river bed recently won, being found to be untenable by day, 2 guns were placed to graze this area, firing from the N. slope of the valley towards CROISILLES. These were in position by 10 P.M.	AL
do	22		Heavy rain until late afternoon. A Sec. relieved by C Sec. & went out to B Echelon. One gun of B Sec. placed near PUG lane, to guard our left front.	AL
do	23		All quiet except for the usual shelling on both sides. One gun near the River Road prepared for sniping against the enemy on the opposite ridge.	AL
do	24		3 guns relieved by No. 55 M.G.Coy; movement on that Bde. side - stopping into our area. These guns kept in the tunnel after which, to be used in case of alarm.	

Army Form C. 2118.

WAR DIARY
INTELLIGENCE SUMMARY.
(Erase heading not required.)

Instructions regarding War Diaries and Intelligence Summaries are contained in F. S. Regs., Part II. and the Staff Manual respectively. Title pages will be prepared in manuscript.

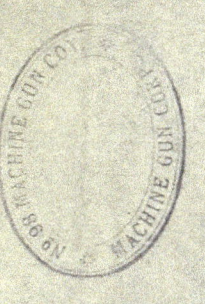

Place	Date	Hour	Summary of Events and Information	Remarks and references to Appendices
Tunnel Off. FONTAINE	MAY 1917 25		Lieut. T. ROBERTS reported for duty from Base Depôt. The day was quiet except for artillery activity. Lieut. Ockenden took over C Sec. from Lieut. Atherton, who went to B Echelon. Enemy aircraft dropped bombs about 10 p.m. No results.	A1.
do.	26		Lieut. Atherton proceeded on leave to England. 3 emplacements completed for delivering direct barrage fire, near FOP Lane. Emplacement constructed during the night near RIVER ROAD, but not occupied.	A1.
do.	27		At 1.55 p.m. an intense bombardment of the HINDENBURG (TUNNEL) line S. of the river SENSEE. At 2 p.m. 98th & 24 Bde attacked up the hill from the river bed & secured a block-house on the FONTAINE – CROISILLES road. The attack by 19th Bde on the right was held up. One gun was rushed to a prepared emplacement on RIVER ROAD, to guard against attack from the village, the NCO i/c, L/Cpl. RIDER, exhibiting a good grasp of the situation. This gun remained in a permanent defensive position. For 45 mins. after Zero 4 guns put down an indirect barrage on the W. side of FONTAINE village, & for 5 mins. after zero TUNNEL Trench was enfiladed by 3 guns firing direct from the opposite slope. The attack was not continued further, & the captured blockhouse was consolidated.	A1.
do.	28		A Sec. relieved D Sec. in reserve. D Sec. relieved C Sec. in front line. Relief complete 6 a.m. A quiet day. Lieut. W.K. Rennie proceeded on leave to England. No. 70740 Pte. Bryce W. accidentally killed. 	A1.

WAR DIARY
INTELLIGENCE SUMMARY.
(Erase heading not required.)

Army Form C. 2118.

Place	Date	Hour	Summary of Events and Information	Remarks and references to Appendices
Trenches at FONTAINE	MAY 1917 29		Very quiet in the line. Nothing of importance occurred.	A.L.
do.	30		Heavy thunderstorms in the afternoon. O.C. 64 M.G. Coy reconnoitred the line & arranged details of relief.	A.L.
do.	31		Coy. was relieved in the line by No. 64 M.G. Coy., relief commencing at 2 P.M. Relief complete 10·30 A.M. Coy proceeded after relief to BLAIREVILLE, arriving about 1·30 P.M. & billeted in huts in a quarry on E. side of village.	A.L.

Ahonat Lieut
Comdg No. 98 M.G. Coy

No. 98
MACHINE GUN
COMPANY.
No. ....
Date 1-7-17

CONFIDENTIAL.

Vol 14

War Diary

of

No. 98 Machine Gun Company

for the

Month of June 1917.

WAR DIARY or INTELLIGENCE SUMMARY

Army Form C. 2118.

No. 93 MACHINE GUN COMPANY.

Place	Date	Hour	Summary of Events and Information	Remarks and references to Appendices
BLAIREVILLE	1/6/17		Company cleaned frames & gun equipment. Gas helmets were inspected by the Coy N.C.O. Billets were improved & Company paid out	JRO
BLAIREVILLE	2/6/17		Boltes were taken during the day. During the morning two hours technical training was done. Section arrangements written. Continued extremely hot.	JRO
BLAIREVILLE	3/6/17		Church Parade for R.C., C. of E. & voluntary services were held. 2 O.R.s reported for duty from Base Depot.	JRO
BLAIREVILLE	4/6/17		Armourer Sergt of 4th Suffolks inspected all arms of the Company. Subsequently limber wagons were washed. Lt. A. LOMAX left for U.K. on leave. Lt. T.M. OKENDEN took over command of the Company. Divisional Band played in camp during afternoon.	JRO
BLAIREVILLE	5/6/17		Morning spent in arms drill & cleaning S.A.A. in belts & scrubbing belts	JRO
BLAIREVILLE	6/6/17		Remainder of belts scrubbed & rifles & limbers wagons greased. A court-martial arrived in on of the Coy billets. Pte BUCK tried by C.M. Pte BRYCE - case adjourned. Weather continues extremely hot. Thunderstorm in evening	JRO

Army Form C. 2118.

No. 93
MACHINE GUN COMPANY.

WAR DIARY
or
INTELLIGENCE SUMMARY
(Erase heading not required.)

Instructions regarding War Diaries and Intelligence Summaries are contained in F. S. Regs., Part II. and the Staff Manual respectively. Title pages will be prepared in manuscript.

Place	Date	Hour	Summary of Events and Information	Remarks and references to Appendices
BLAIREVILLE	7/6/17		Training employed in Arms drill & Lewis training. Afternoon heavy thunderstorm. Lt A W HARTHORN left for U.K. on leave.	JAD
do	8/6/17		Morning spent in Arms drill and Lewis training. 1 O.R. evacuated. Lieut C.S. HEDGELAND from M.G. School & Lieut PRATHERTON from leave U.K. who latter takes over command.	RMG
do	9/6/17		M.G. Drill & gun instruction.	RMG
do	10/6/17		Church parade in morning. Lieut W.K. RENNIE returned from leave to U.K.	RMG
do	11/6/17		M.G. Drill. Major C.D.JAY awarded D.S.O., LT. C.S HEDGELAND mentioned in despatches	RMG
do	12/6/17		During morning company paraded for baths. In the afternoon some very successful company sports were held, a section competition for a very popular Order of finishing was: C Sec, B Sec, Transport Headquarters, D Sec, A Sec. 235 francs expended in prizes in the form of credits on the company canteen. LT. T D SHERRIFF left for U.K. on leave. Sergt BAXTER to 123 M G Coy to be C.Q.M.S.	C.S. H.
do	13/6/17		Arms drill, short mile march and lecture on German machine gun. In afternoon a football match v 2nd Argylls was lost 9-1	C.S.H.
do	14/6/17		Physical training, loading pack mules and firing on range. 1 O.R evacuated to hospital.	C.S.H.

WAR DIARY
or
INTELLIGENCE SUMMARY.
(Erase heading not required.)

Army Form C. 2118.

No. 253 MACHINE GUN COMPANY.

Instructions regarding War Diaries and Intelligence Summaries are contained in F. S. Regs., Part II. and the Staff Manual respectively. Title pages will be prepared in manuscript.

Place	Date	Hour	Summary of Events and Information	Remarks and references to Appendices
BLAIREVILLE	15/6/17		Firing on range, barrage drill + revolver exercises. In the afternoon a cricket match v 1st Middx. 2Lt F.W.BRICKELL on transport course at ABBEVILLE. 5 OR returned from leave.	Cas. Nil
do	16/6/17		Ammo drill, barrage drill + lectures.	Cas. Nil
do	17/6/17		Medal distribution by G.O.C. VIth Corps, followed by Church service. The following received the Military Medal for gallantry in action. 70331 Corpl HARRIS W., 70736 L/Corpl MOORCROFT A., 70745 L/Corpl WILSON T., L/Corpl LOMAX (from leave) took over command.	Cas. Nil
do	18/6/17		Changing ammunition in belts and inspection for rivets. During the rest at BLAIREVILLE the company canteen made a profit of 400 francs (approx.) which went to the sports fund. In the evening the company left BLAIREVILLE, bivouacked for two hours at BOYELLES where the sections had a meal before proceeding to trenches.	Cas. Nil
BOYELLES Trenches at FONTAINE les-CROISILLES	19	1AM	Relief of No.14 M.G. Coy commenced. Dispositions - guns Frontline, 3 guns in action, 2 in reserve; Support - 3 guns; Reserve 4 guns. One section in Bde. reserve at B Echelon, BOYELLES. Relief complete 6AM.	AZ

WAR DIARY or INTELLIGENCE SUMMARY

Army Form C. 2118.

No. 99 MACHINE GUN COMPANY.

Place	Date June 1917	Hour	Summary of Events and Information	Remarks and references to Appendices
Trenches S/o FONTAINE	20		Commenced today, bombardments are carried out daily on enemy's trenches from 11 to 12 noon & 7 to 8 p.m. Lieut Hatcham returns from leave to UK	AL
do	21		All quiet in the line. Very little shelling on either side	AL
do	22		Lieut Ockenden left on leave for UK. 2/Lt. I Roberts evacuated sick & struck off the strength.	AL
do	23	8pm	C. Sec. relieved D. Sec. & D. Sec. relieved A. Sec. At 12 midnight 19th Bde. attacked a portion of Tunnel Trench, 500 yds S.W. of FONTAINE but 2 guns A.Sec. & 6 guns 150th M.G. Coy. came under the tactical orders of the A.L. Coy, providing indirect fire on enemy Comm. trenches.	AL
do	24	8am	A. Sec. relieved B. Sec. B. Sec. remained during the day & night in the trenches, in readiness for an attack by 100th Bde. in the morning.	AL
do	25		100th Bde. attack cancelled. B. Sec. returned to B Echelon at 8 am	AL
do	26	1am 12.30	10th Div. attacked enemy trench N.W. of FONTAINE WOOD. Attack successful. 6 guns of 100th M.G. Coy were firing from this Bde. area on the S.E. edge of the wood. Lieut T.D Sherriff returned from leave to UK 3 days overdue owing to delays.	AL

WAR DIARY
or
INTELLIGENCE SUMMARY.
(Erase heading not required.)

Army Form C. 2118.

No. 98 MACHINE GUN COMPANY.

Place	Date 1917	Hour	Summary of Events and Information	Remarks and references to Appendices
Trenches opp. FONTAINE	June 27		A quiet day. Lieut. Sherriff took over command of D. Sec. in support position & 2/Lt. Marshall went to C. Sec. in reserve. (Bombardment of enemy trenches).	A.L.
do.	28		Heavy bombardment continued till early morning; but no enemy attack developed on our Bde. front. On front line position were damaged, but no casualties to Ella guns or personnel. 2/Lt. Marshall went to A Sec. in front line for instruction. Very heavy thunderstorm about 7.30 P.M.	A.L.
do.	29		O.C. 62 M.G. Coy. reported at 3.30 p.m. to arrange details of relief. At 8.50 A.M. 100 B Bde. on our right attacked a portion of Tunnel Trench, but was unsuccessful. Indirect fire was placed by B. Sec. on an area W. of FONTAINE in support of the attack – Enemy retaliation very carried on intermittently until 12 noon. Enemy shelled from FIT Lane to the river SENSEE heavy about noon. Especially from FIT Lane to the river SENSEE. Lieut. A. LOMAX appointed to command this unit (Authy VII Corps wire A/631 dated 29th June) vice Major C.D. JAY, D.S.O. evacuated 28 June 1917.	A.L.
do.	30		Coy relief by 62 M.G. Coy. commenced at 5 p.m. & complete at 10.30 p.m. D Sec. in support evacuated their positions at 10 p.m by arrangement with relieving Coy. Transport of B Sec. proceeded by road to BAILLEULVAL at 10 A.M. The last Plan of Coy after relief entrained at BOYELLES at 2 A.M. 30 June 1st July, & joined the transport at BAILLEULVAL at 6 A.M. 1st July.	A.L.

A. Romax Capt
Cmdg. No. 98 M.G. Coy.

"A" Form.
MESSAGES AND SIGNALS.

Army Form C. 2121.

Prefix......Code......m.	Words	Charge	This message is on a/c of:	Recd. at......m.
Office of Origin and Service Instructions.	Sent		..........Service.	Date.........
	At......m.			From.........
	To			
	By		(Signature of "Franking Officer.")	By.........

TO	98th Inf. Brigade

Sender's Number.	Day of Month.	In reply to Number.	
* M.G. 350	2nd	BM 38	AAA

Herewith Casualties as requested

22851 Pte HEATH. C. Wounded in Action 22-6-17 (shell fire)

88429 " CHARLES. E. Wounded in action 28-6-17 (G.S.W) rejoined for duty the following day

C.S. Hedgeland Lt.
Adjt 98th M.G. Coy

From 98. M.G. Coy
Place
Time

The above may be forwarded as now corrected. (Z)

Censor. Signature of Addresser or person authorised to telegraph in his name.
* This line should be erased if not required.

No. 98 MACHINE GUN COY.
2-8-17
MACHINE GUN CORPS.

CONFIDENTIAL

Vol 15

War Diary

of

No. 98 Machine Gun Company

for the

Month of July 1917

Army Form C. 2118.

WAR DIARY
INTELLIGENCE SUMMARY.
(Erase heading not required.)

Instructions regarding War Diaries and Intelligence Summaries are contained in F. S. Regs., Part II. and the Staff Manual respectively. Title pages will be prepared in manuscript.

Place	Date	Hour	Summary of Events and Information	Remarks and references to Appendices
BAILLEUVAL	JULY 1st 1917	6.0 A.M.	Arrived at 6 A.M.; after a weary day & train journey & taken up by a relief in trenches to BEAUMETZ. Sleep was permitted till 2 p.m. when cleaning up &c was carried on. Coy was paid at 5.30 p.m.	AL.
	2		The Coy paraded at 9.30 A.M. Capt LOMAX made a short address on assuming command. Remainder of the morning spent in packing limbers, cleaning guns &c.	AL.
	3		Moved off at 6.30 A.M. for ACHEUX, via BAILLEULMONT, LA CAUCHIE, HENU & AUTHIE. Arrived at ACHEUX 1.30 P.M. Marched through great heat & over bad roads. 7 men fell out & reported sick.	AL.
ACHEUX	4		Left ACHEUX 5.50 A.M. for TALMAS, via PUCHEVILLERS & VAL de MAISON. March complete 9.15 A.M. One man fell out. Sick men from previous march were carried in a lorry. Rainy & oppressive during the march. Roads very bad.	AL.
TALMAS	5		Left at 4.50 A.M. for BELLOY-sur-SOMME, via NAOURS and VIGNACOURT. March complete 11 A.M. No one fell out on line of march. Very hot weather. 1 O.R. evacuated sick.	AL.
BELLOY SUR SOMME	6		Left at 5.20 A.M. for AVE LESGES, via BOURDON, HANGEST, SOUES, LE QUESNOY. March complete 11.15 A.M.	AL.

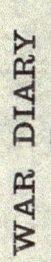

WAR DIARY
INTELLIGENCE SUMMARY

Army Form C. 2118.

Place	Date	Hour	Summary of Events and Information	Remarks and references to Appendices
AVELESGES	July 1917 7		Cleaning up in morning. In afternoon, Lindsay received Lt. J.R. OCKENDEN reported for leave to UK 2 O.R. reported from CAMIERS convoe.	AL
	8	AM 10.45	C of E Parade at WARLUS.	AL
	9		Parade from 7AM to 12.30 pm. commenced & continued daily throughout the training period. Lectures given on fire direction.	AL
	10		Training proceeded with. A lorry to AMIENS every Monday & Friday, in which 3 vacancies are given to the Coy. 2/Lt. MARSHALL began a course for range-takers. Lieut J.R. OCKENDEN appointed to command "A" Sec.	AL
	11	11 AM	Divisional commander, accompanied by G.O.C. 98th Inf. Bde. visited the Coy., and watched the training for a short time. Major EDJAY DSO. M.C. the Off. Mess	AL
	12		Training in Gun drill and indirect fire practice.	AL
	13		Divl Band gave a concert at 3pm on the village Green. Major JAY left for Base Depôt after conducting his short visit to the Coy.	AL
	14		Usual training proceeded with. Lt. R.R. ATHERTON to PARIS-PLAGE on 6 days leave	AL

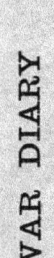

Army Form C. 2118.

WAR DIARY
or
INTELLIGENCE SUMMARY.
(Erase heading not required.)

Instructions regarding War Diaries and Intelligence Summaries are contained in F. S. Regs., Part II. and the Staff Manual respectively. Title pages will be prepared in manuscript.

Place	Date	Hour	Summary of Events and Information	Remarks and references to Appendices
AVELESGES	July 1917 15	11 AM	C. of E. Parade at WARLUS.	AZ
		2.30 pm	Played at hockey, cricket, & later after a clock contest game hence J.D.O. COATS and 3/Lt. F.S.J. ADAMS reported for duty from Base Depot & were posted respectively to A & C Secns.	
	16		Revolver exercises & machine gun range practice. The Div¹ concert party entertainment in the village given at 7 pm. 2Lt. A.W. HARTSHORN to D See as out-section Offr. 1 O.R. evacuated sick.	AZ
	17		5 O.R. reported from Base Depot. Coy bathed between 11 & 1 pm.	AZ
	18		Range practice (B Sec). Lt. C.S. HEDGELAND appointed 2nd in command (A.G. A/15908/427) (from 13/7/17) 1 O.R. evacuated sick.	AZ
	19	10 AM 10.45 11.15	The O.C. inspected the Coy. in full marching order. Inspection of billets. Inspection of guns and section-stores.	AZ
	20	6 AM	The O.C. & Lt. SHERRIFF left to take part in a Divisional exercise without troops in the area between ARRAINES and AMIENS. 8 Infantry Officers were attached to sections during morning parades for instructional purposes. Played 4th Suff R¹ at cricket & won.	AZ

WAR DIARY
or
INTELLIGENCE SUMMARY.

Army Form C. 2118.

Place	Date	Hour	Summary of Events and Information	Remarks and references to Appendices
AVELESGES	July 1917 21	AM 4.15 4 pm	Route march - BELLOY - DROMESNIL - SELINCOURT - AUMONT. Pte. OC & Lt. SHERRIFF returned from Divisional exercise. Lt Atherton reported from leave 26.7.17	AL
do	22		Church parade at WARLUS at 11 AM.	AL
do	23		Section training round the billets. 1 OR from Base Depot. 1 OR to Base	AL
do	24	7 AM 2 pm	Route march - BELLOY - St MALVIS - LE CHAUSSOY. The OC lectured on lesson learnt during recent divisional exercise	AL
do	25		Range practice and map-reading during the morning.	AL
do	26		Range practice and map reading.	AL
do	27	7.30 AM 2 pm	Route march - MONTAGNE - MOLLIENS - Vidame - CAMPS-en-Amienois. The OC inspected the Coy Transport. 9782 C.S.M. GENDERS. W. + 26550 Sgt JONES. A. left for Base to take up commissioned rank. 18827 CQMS Scott Temp. CSM - 22635 Sgt Waddell L temp. CQMS	AL
do	28		Box respirator drill, & interval economy during the morning. 1 OR rejoined from CAMIERS. (M.G. School)	AL
do	29		C of E. Church parade prevented by heavy storms, which continued until late afternoon.	AL

Army Form C. 2118.

WAR DIARY
INTELLIGENCE SUMMARY.
(Erase heading not required.)

Place	Date	Hour	Summary of Events and Information	Remarks and references to Appendices
AVELESGES	1917 JULY 30	12 noon	Section training carried on during the morning. Billetting party (Lt. Atherton & 2 OR) left LONGPRE station to arrange for billetting of the Coy. at new destination.	AZ
do	31	AM 5·0	The Coy. moved off for AVELESGES, arriving at LONGPRE at 8.15 AM. At 9.41 AM. train moved off, and proceeded via CALAIS and DUNKERQUE to ADINKERKE, arriving about 6.30 P.M. Detrainment complete at 9.40 P.M., at which time moved off for LA PANNE, where the Coy. was accommodated in hutments in the sand dunes. March complete 10.45 P.M.	AZ

A. Kumar Capt.
Commanding No. 98 M. G. Coy.

Vol 16

War Diary
of
No 98 Machine Gun Company
for the
Month of August 1917

No. 98
MACHINE GUN
COMPANY.
No.
Date. 2-9-17

Army Form C. 2118.

No. 98
MACHINE GUN
COMPANY.

WAR DIARY
INTELLIGENCE SUMMARY.
(Erase heading not required.)

Instructions regarding War Diaries and Intelligence Summaries are contained in F. S. Regs. Part II. and the Staff Manual respectively. Title pages will be prepared in manuscript.

Place	Date 1917	Hour	Summary of Events and Information	Remarks and references to Appendices
LA PANNE BAINS	Aug 1		Cleaning equipment, limbers &c. The Coy. billeted in hutments off the FURNES road., ½ mile East of LA PANNE. Officers mess at Western end of the DIGUE.	AL
do	2		Bn. placed under 6 hours notice to move to the trench-area. Morning parades & inspections as usual. Bathing parade in the sea commenced & carried on throughout the stay at LA PANNE.	AL
do	3		Training carried on during the morning. No event of importance occurred. Two gun numbers seen the camp for anti aircraft rifle.	AL
do	4		Training in billets as usual.	AL
do	5	AM 8.30 9.0 2pm	Church parade in English Church near hospital. R.C. service at R.C. Church. Lieut. A.W. HARTSHORN & 2 NCOs left for Depot Battn. GHYVELDE, for gas course. 3 O.R. departed on leave for UK.	AL
do	6		A & C Sections fired on the sands. Remainder of Coy. engaged in usual training routine. Lt. COATS & 2 NCOs left for Anti Aircraft Course at BRAY Dunes.	AL
do	7		Firing - instruction with American Army Screen Training as usual. 4 O.R. reinforcements reported from Base Depot.	AL

WAR DIARY
or
INTELLIGENCE SUMMARY.
(Erase heading not required.)

Army Form C. 2118.

No. 98 MACHINE GUN COMPANY

Place	Date 1917	Hour	Summary of Events and Information	Remarks and references to Appendices
LA PANNE BAINS	Aug 8	AM 10	The Coy. witnessed a Contact Control Scheme carried out in LA PANNE West Training Area. 5 O.R. departed on leave to U.K. 2 O.R. left for Base Depot (inefficient).	AL
do	9		Usual training in the morning. C.S.M. Scott A. promoted to C.S.M. & to serve with the unit.	AL
do	10		Training in Barrage Drill throughout the morning. Lieut HARTSHORN & 2 O.R. returned from Gas Course.	AL
do	11		Interior Economy. 1 O.R. (Acting Cook) left for 21 days Cookery Course at ZUYDCOOTE.	AL
do	12	AM 10 9	C. of E. service in English Church. R.C. service in R.C. Church. Lieut W.K. RENNIE, C.S.M. Scott & Sgt MOORE left for Anti aircraft course at BRAY DUNES.	AL
do	13		Barrage - drill exercises. Sgt Tookey acting CSM during temporary absence of C.S.M. Scott.	AL
do	14	AM 8 to 1pm	Firing practices in LA PANNE Northern Area West.	AL

WAR DIARY or INTELLIGENCE SUMMARY

Army Form C. 2118.

No. 98 MACHINE GUN COMPANY.

Place	Date	Hour	Summary of Events and Information	Remarks and references to Appendices
LA PANNE BAINS	AUGUST 1917 15		Section training. Lieut RENNIE & 2 O.R. rejoined from A.A. course. 5 O.R. left for leave to U.K.	AL
do.	16	AM 5.50	Moved off for COXYDE, arriving 7.30 AM. COXYDE - COXYDE BAINS road. Lieut C.S. HEDGELAND and 2/Lieut. C.L. MARSHALL departed on leave to UK. C.Q.M.S. THORNCROFT reported for duty.	AL
COXYDE Rt.	17		The O.C. & 2 officers reconnoitred positions to be taken over in the trenches, and made arrangements for relief.	AL
do	18	PM 6.0	Left COXYDE by sections, & proceeded via WULPEN Bridge to PELICAN BRIDGE, S. of NIEUPORT, where limbers were sent back. Relieved No. 96 M.G. Coy. in positions along BRUGES road. Relief complete 12 midnight. Dispositions – 8 guns near junction of RAMSCAPELLE and BRUGES road; 4 guns along YSER canal; 4 guns behind St. GEORGES, all firing on S.O.S. lines at about 2000x range.	AL
Trenches	19		Considerable shelling, particularly of NIEUPORT and the bridges. All quiet at the positions.	AL

Army Form C. 2118.

No. 98
MACHINE GUN COMPANY.

WAR DIARY
or
INTELLIGENCE SUMMARY.
(Erase heading not required.)

Instructions regarding War Diaries and Intelligence Summaries are contained in F.S. Regs., Part II. and the Staff Manual respectively. Title pages will be prepared in manuscript.

Place	Date	Hour	Summary of Events and Information	Remarks and references to Appendices
Trenches	August 1917 20		Artillery very active on both sides. Slight shelling of our centre positions by Minenwerfer. 3500 rounds fired during the night on enemy trenches.	AL
do	21	6pm	Artillery fire still very heavy. One YSER Canal position shelled with 5.9" hows. 10 R. wounded. 6000 rounds fired on various targets throughout the night.	AL
do	22		Hostile shelling still heavy. 4000 rounds fired on enemy trenches throughout the night.	AL
do	23	7pm	YSER Canal and BRUGES road positions shelled with shrapnel & small calibre HE. No casualties.	AL
do	24	8AM	C. Sec. withdrawn to Coy HQ. to act as a reserve for the YSER line E & of Cuy Ponts. Movement complete 11 AM. 2 new positions occupied on YSER Canal. Present dispositions: 6 guns along YSER canal front on to LOMBARTZYDE: 3 guns on BRUGES road and 3 guns near NASTY WALK, behind ST. GEORGES.	AL

Army Form C. 2118.

No. 98
MACHINE GUN COMPANY
No. ....
Date ....

WAR DIARY
or
INTELLIGENCE SUMMARY.
(Erase heading not required.)

Instructions regarding War Diaries and Intelligence Summaries are contained in F.S. Regs., Part II. and the Staff Manual respectively. Title pages will be prepared in manuscript.

Place	Date AUGUST 1917	Hour	Summary of Events and Information	Remarks and references to Appendices
Trenches	25	12 m.d.	All quiet in the line. Sec Enemy 2nd A&SH attempted a raid on ROSE trench, but it was unsuccessful. We supplied flanking overhead fire on communication trenches in rear, & engaged neighbouring bridges over the NIEUWENDAMME brook.	A2.
"	26.		Usual indirect fire was carried out on enemy trenches. Heavy shelling near Coy H.Q.	M&R
"	27.		At 1a.m. a Trench hunter Gun Nortonbridge was carried out on Bug Front & Germs assisted with Indirect fire on Pt Hrs. of positn being bombarded. Usual Indirect fire was carried out during the day. 1 O.R Killed. 2 O.R Wounded.	M&R
"	28.	10 a.m.	O.C. 97th M.G Coy visited Coy H.Q. Trench armament for relief. On the night 28/9 Coy was relieved by 97th Coy. 3 Sections in the line, 1 at Coy H.Q	M&R
COXYDE	29		Coy marched to COXYDE. At 12 m.n. Coy left for BRAY DUNES.	M&R
BRAY DUNES.	30.		Day was spent Cleaning Guns, Equipment &c.	M&R

Army Form C. 2118.

WAR DIARY
or
INTELLIGENCE SUMMARY.
(Erase heading not required.)

No. 98 MACHINE GUN COMPANY.

Place	Date	Hour	Summary of Events and Information	Remarks and references to Appendices
BRAY DUNES.	31		Transport left for SALPERWICK at 10-0 a.m. Lieut COATS accompanied them. Coy spent day cleaning up	WWR

M.R.W.........Capt.
Commanding No. 98 M. G. Coy.

CONFIDENTIAL

Vol 17

War Diary of
9th Machine Gun Company
for the Month of September 1917.

WAR DIARY
or
INTELLIGENCE SUMMARY.
(Erase heading not required.)

Army Form C. 2118.

Place	Date	Hour	Summary of Events and Information	Remarks and references to Appendices
BRAY DUNES	SEPT 1st		Left BRAY DUNES by train and detrained AUDRUICQ. Marched to SALPERWICK, near ST. OMER, where the company O.R. encamped.	C.S.H.
SALPERWICK	2nd		General cleaning up.	C.S.H.
"	3rd		Baths. 2nd C.S. HEDGELAND returned from leave to U.K. and took over command	C.S.H.
"	4th		Training in billets. Two guns mounted for aircraft firing. Four four consecutive nights ST. OMER & neighbourhood were bombed by German aeroplanes.	C.S.H.
"	5th		Pontoon work. 5 O.Rs reported from Base Depot. 1 O.R. evacuated.	C.S.H.
WATTEN	6th		Moved to new billets at WATTEN. Inter-brigade football competition was decided on.	C.S.H.
"	7th		Training in billets.	C.S.H.

WAR DIARY or INTELLIGENCE SUMMARY

Army Form C. 2118.

Place	Date	Hour	Summary of Events and Information	Remarks and references to Appendices
WATTEN	8th		Training & Bath Parade.	C.S.M.
	9th		Training & bomb throwing. Wire & wire fixing. Football.	C.S.M.
	10th		Bath in 94th Field Ambulance. Section training including tactical exercises in open warfare. Football match v 2nd I.O.R. evacuated to C.C.S.	C.S.M.
	11th		Section training & bathing. Lt. R.R. ATHERTON promoted on leave to U.K. and Lt. W.R. RENNIE took over duties of 2nd in command. Weekly allotment of leave vacancies now 3 O.R.'s. from men then attaining ship who came out with the original company to act as first leave.	C.S.M.
	12th		Barrage Platoons. 1 O.R. invalided from Base Depot.	C.S.M.
	13th		Lectures. Range work. Sect. & Coy in attacking Pl. 1 O.R. evacuated (sick) Football match v 4th Kings Liverpool Regt. Lt. W.R. RENNIE on leave. Lt. J.R. OLKENDEN 2nd in command	C.S.M.

Army Form C. 2118.

WAR DIARY
or
INTELLIGENCE SUMMARY.
(Erase heading not required.)

Instructions regarding War Diaries and Intelligence Summaries are contained in F. S. Regs., Part II. and the Staff Manual respectively. Title pages will be prepared in manuscript.

Place	Date	Hour	Summary of Events and Information	Remarks and references to Appendices
WATTEN	14th		Series Training. Football match v 4th Suffolk Regt. won by the company 1-0.	C.S.H.
NORDPEENE	15th		Marched to NORDPEENE. Passed G.O.C. Division on line of march.	C.S.H.
STEENVORDE	16th		Marched to STEENVORDE – Bizarre billet for the night in a farm about 2 miles from the town – 2 sections under canvas. 10.R. evacuated.	C.S.H.
BERTHEN	17th		Marched to BERTHEN. During the three days march no men fell out.	C.S.H.
"	18th		Outer audium open equipment.	Cont'd
"	19th		Series Training. Lecture "Lessons from the attack" for all ranks by O.C. 1st Middx Regt.	C.S.H.
RENINGHELST	20th		Marched to RENINGHELST. Billeted in ONTARIO CAMP. Lt. HARTSHORN to hosp.	C.S.H.

WAR DIARY
or
INTELLIGENCE SUMMARY.

(Erase heading not required.)

Army Form C. 2118.

Instructions regarding War Diaries and Intelligence Summaries are contained in F. S. Regs., Part II. and the Staff Manual respectively. Title pages will be prepared in manuscript.

Place	Date	Hour	Summary of Events and Information	Remarks and references to Appendices
RENINGHELST	21/9/17		Preparation for line. Lectures to officers N.C.Os. Congress at Proged. Headquarters bombing by hostile aeroplane at night.	C.R.Q.
RENINGHELST	22/9/17		S.O.R. attached from each battalion to observers. Some large rations moved to each man.	C.R.Q.
RAILWAY DUGOUTS	23/9/17		Batt. moved to RAILWAY EMBANKMENT DUGOUTS preparatory to their Spent the night in some old gun pits. Transport & B Echelon from DICKEBUSCH	C.R.Q.
TRENCHES	24/9/17		O.C. went up to take over from 60 n G.R. at 6 am. Sections followed, the first reaching at 11 a m. The Brigade front extended from POLYGON WOOD to R., REUTEL BEEK. Two guns were in position near VELDHOEK FARM, two at FITZCLARENCE. Three near A.S. Given. B.E. sections remained in reserve at	C.R.Q.
GHEWELT			STIRLING CASTLE and CLAPHAM JUNCTION respectively ready to go forward with the assaulting infantry. The O.C. of the battalion to which they were to be attached was seen & half-actions were made. Relief complete 6pm no casualties. Ammunition	

A5834 Wt. W4973/M687 750,000 8/16 D. D. & L. Ltd. Forms/C.2118/13.

Army Form C. 2118.

WAR DIARY
or
INTELLIGENCE SUMMARY.
(Erase heading not required.)

Instructions regarding War Diaries and Intelligence Summaries are contained in F. S. Regs., Part II. and the Staff Manual respectively. Title pages will be prepared in manuscript.

Place	Date	Hour	Summary of Events and Information	Remarks and references to Appendices
TRENCHES	25/9/17		shelling at night when the infantry were relieved. Before the relief of the infantry front line battalion (1st Brade) was complete the enemy attacked under cover of the early morning mist and inflicted severe casualties. The attack was strong and vigorous and throughout the day fighting continued with varying fortune. The 2 guns at VELDHOEK FARM came into action & inflicted considerable damage on the enemy apparently advancing at KEIBERG mols. The enemy knowing our this traversed the ground had our experienced and lasted from dawn until 2 h.m. but were not heavily shelled. Casualties – 5 O.R.s wounded (shell). The attack ordered for the 26th when to be carried out then relieves Brigade (10th) together with the 4th Suffolks to undertake the attack. B Section (4 guns) were attached to the 3rd Scottish Rifles, C Section (4 guns) to the 4th Suffolk Regt. B Section moved off at 8.30 pm.	ES M
TRENCHES	26/9/17		Zero 5.50 am. At 4.10 am the 5th Scottish Rifles were in JASPER AVENUE having lost touch with guns. They moved off again to assemble point at 4.30 am. B Section was unable to keep touch & remained in JASPER AVENUE. C Sction ...	ES M

Army Form C. 2118.

WAR DIARY
or
INTELLIGENCE SUMMARY.
(Erase heading not required.)

Instructions regarding War Diaries and Intelligence Summaries are contained in F. S. Regs., Part II. and the Staff Manual respectively. Title pages will be prepared in manuscript.

Place	Date	Hour	Summary of Events and Information	Remarks and references to Appendices
			to FITZCLARENCE FARM. Before zero a heavy barrage was put down in the area and dropped the attack. One gun of C Section knocked out. The Suffolks suffered heavy casualties - after them went forward the situation was obscure. C Section 3 guns were ordered to take up defensive position on the FITZCLARENCE FARM Line. One gun of A Section had also been put out of action. Meanwhile the 2 guns near VELDHOEK FARM had been doing good work all day engaging targets. D Section's seven sections were fired at & were to crawl in POLYGON WOOD. Casualties Killed 10.R., wounded 30.R., missing 31.Rs.	C.S.M
TRENCHES	27.9.17		Trench's continued all day. News that situation was not thought established. Relief arrived 69 B? taking over. Relief complete 7.30 p.m. Company spent night in RAILWAY DUGOUTS. Casualties Killed 10.R, wounded 10.R. wounded 2.O.R. (1 believed killed). Killed 2.O.Rs, wounded 11.O.R. (3 believed killed). Total Casualties 27.9.17 killed 2.O.Rs (1 believed killed). Missing 2.O.Rs (1 believed killed), by these wounded men — wounded 3 missing.	C.S.q

WAR DIARY
or
INTELLIGENCE SUMMARY.
(Erase heading not required.)

Army Form C. 2118.

Instructions regarding War Diaries and Intelligence Summaries are contained in F. S. Regs., Part II. and the Staff Manual respectively. Title pages will be prepared in manuscript.

Place	Date	Hour	Summary of Events and Information	Remarks and references to Appendices
HALLOY SUZUTE	27.9.17		In morning remainder of parade attended to EBBLINGHEM. Capt A LOMAX to leave after further exam at G.H.Q. Lnck Corm School attached not returned to battalion.	Ex. M
EBBLINGHEM	29.9.17		Transport moved off at 9.0am. Confirm move to 2 Echelon, thence to EBBLINGHEM (by tram).	OUEDROM Ex. A
"	30.9.17		Showers at intervals. Letters fair but unsettled. Lt. COATS and 2 O.Rs transferred to 201 Coy	Ex. 16

C.S. Adjutant Lt.

Army Form C. 2118.

WAR DIARY
or
INTELLIGENCE SUMMARY.
(Erase heading not required.)

WD 15

CONFIDENTIAL

War Diary of No. 98 Machine Gun Company
from 1st to 31st October 1917

No. 98 MACHINE GUN COY. — MACHINE GUN CORPS.

Place	Date	Hour	Summary of Events and Information	Remarks and references to Appendices

WAR DIARY
or
INTELLIGENCE SUMMARY

Army Form C. 2118.

Place	Date	Hour	Summary of Events and Information	Remarks and references to Appendices
RENESCURE	OCT 1917 1		Anti-gas drill & general inspection & kit during the morning. Congratulations from G.O.C.-in-C received for recent operation. Casualties (total) Officers - NIL, O.R. 2 killed, 11 wounded, 5 missing. Lieut. J.D.O. COATS + 4 O.R. transferred & proceeded to 207 M.G. Coy.	A1.
do.	2		Cleaning-up continued. 5 O.R. to U.K on leave	A1.
do.	3	AM 10.30	Inspected by J.M. Sir D HAIG. Baths in the afternoon. 8 O.R. reported from Base Depot.	A1.
do.	4		Lt. Sherriff & 5 O.R. on leave to U.K. 32 men attached to the Coy from Battns. in the Brigade. Draft of attached men inspected by O.C. 2/Lt. Adam left for leave to U.K.	A1.
	5	8.30 AM	moved to HALLINES. Arrived 12 noon.	A1.
HALLINES	6		moved to NEUVE EGLISE, transport by road. Personnel entrained at WIZERNES at about 2 p.m. & detrained at BAILLEUL about 10.30 P.M. Arrived at camp about 12 midnight	A1.
NEUVE EGLISE	7		Coy. rested during the morning. Football in the afternoon. 2 O.R. returned from leave to U.K.	A1.
	8		Indoor training carried on. 4 O.R. reported from leave. 5 O.R. left for leave to U.K. 10 guns (B.C.+D. Secs) proceeded to trenches under 19 M.C. Coy.	A1.

WAR DIARY
or
INTELLIGENCE SUMMARY.

(Erase heading not required.)

Army Form C. 2118.

Place	Date	Hour	Summary of Events and Information	Remarks and references to Appendices
NEUVE EGLISE	OCT 1917 9		Training carried on as usual. Capt. A. LOMAX returned from leave to UK & resumed command.	AL
	10	2.50 pm	Moved to CRUMLIN lines, about 2 hours march. Range finding class commenced under the Marshall.	AL
	11		Training by sections in the morning. Football during the afternoon.	AL
	12		Training as usual.	AL
	13		Training as usual. 3 O.R. to 2nd Army Rest Camp.	AL
	14		C.O.'s parade in the morning.	AL
	15		Work commenced on new lines at BULFORD camp. 4 junior NCOs left for 248 M.G. Coy for a course of ins~. The 10 guns under 19 M.G. Coy were relieved by 110th & 248 M.G. Coy. Relief complete 9 p.m.	AL
	16		Capt. Lomax proceeded to the Div. Artillery for a 4 days course. Teams from trenches cleaned up this morning. At 7/Lt. Adam reported from leave to UK	AL
	17	9.0 am	Coy moved to BULFORD Camp. 15 O.R. returned from Base Depot. 5 O.R. left for leave to UK	AL

Army Form C. 2118.

WAR DIARY
INTELLIGENCE SUMMARY
(Erase heading not required.)

88 MACHINE GUN COY.

Place	Date	Hour	Summary of Events and Information	Remarks and references to Appendices
NEUVE EGLISE	Oct 1917 18		Training as usual. Lt. Hartshorn took over temporarily the duties of Div. Gas Officer. Lt. Ockenden & 2 O.R. proceeded on leave to U.K.	AL
	19		Barrage Drill practice in the morning.	AL
	20		Training as usual. Capt. A. Lomax reported from Artillery course. Cpl. O'Brien, 13470, deprived of stripes by sentence of F.G.C.M. Promulgated at 9.30 A.M.	AL
	21	8 A.M. 9.30	Baths. Capt Dean, H/Cpl Brogan & L/Cpl Campbell awarded M.M. Medal. Church parade. Football in the afternoon.	AL
	22		Revolver practice & aiming instruction. No. 36387 Pte McMahon P. tried by F.G.C.M. The O.C. & 2/Lt. Adams reconnoitred the trenches to be taken over.	AL
	23		During the morning, preparation for the trenches. Sections moves off, commencing 2.45 P.M., at 20 mins. interval in order- A, C, D, B, H.Q.H. Arrived at MESSINES at 5.30 P.M. where relief of 100th M.G. Coy began. A Sec. occupied GAPAARD group, 2 guns of C Sec occupied STEIGNAST FARM, another occupying a position on the opposite bank of the DOUVE river. D See	AL

WAR DIARY / INTELLIGENCE SUMMARY

Army Form C. 2118.

88 MACHINE GUN COY.

Place	Date	Hour	Summary of Events and Information	Remarks and references to Appendices
Trenches opposite MESSINES	1917 OCT 23	7 P.M.	Occupied Support & B Sec. with 18 guns & C Sec. the Reserve positions; 16 guns in the line. Relief, which was quiet, complete about 10 P.M.	AL
do.	24		Occasional shelling of Coy. H.Q. throughout day & night. Indirect fire on selected targets at 6.55 & 7.35 p.m.	AL
do.	25		All quiet in the day. At night active M.G. fire played on Support positions & enfiladed HUNS WALK. 1 O.R. wounded by M.G. fire. Lieut SHERRIFF took over Support position from 2/Lt ADAMS. Harassing fire continued during the night. Rain during night.	AL
do.	26		At dawn 2/Lt ADAMS took over STEIGNAST FARM from Lieut ATHERTON, who then proceeded to BAILLEUL to commence an Anti-Aircraft Course (with 4 O.R.). Heavy rain fell all day, & rendered all work impossible. Enemy very quiet.	AL
do.	27		Urgent protection for anti-gas carried on in M STEIGNAST positions. Day very heavy & misty. Artillery on both sides active about dusk. Enemy M.G. fire active during night on our Support positions.	AL
do.	28	9.45 P.M.	Gas protection completed at STEIGNAST position. Work commenced on a 33 rd Div. Scheme of alternative emplacements. Positions selected & work mapped out. Enemy quiet except at dawn & dusk to KIWI FARM successfully. Enemy much disturbed but little retaliation.	AL

WAR DIARY
or
INTELLIGENCE SUMMARY.

Army Form C. 2118.

Place	Date	Hour	Summary of Events and Information	Remarks and references to Appendices
Trenches near MESSINES	Oct 1917 29	5.15 to 6.0 M	Coy. H.Q. shelled fairly heavily by hostile guns from 7 A.M. to 5 P.M. STEIGNAST was shelled heavily by 5.9 hows. Violently bombarded with arty-harassing fire at 11.55 P.M. GAPAARD positions provided with anti-gas protection. 2/Lt. Arnold left for leave to U.K.	AL
	30		M.G. fire directed on to support positions in early morning. Anti gas protection complete in support positions. O.C. 19th M.G. Coy. arranged details of relief.	AL
	31		GAPAARD positions heavily shelled from 9 A.M. to 4 P.M. Otherwise quiet during the day. Relief by No 9 M.G. Coy commenced 5 P.M. & completed 7.45 P.M. Guns etc were taken out to WULVERGHEM by light tramway. 3 casualties (wounded) sustained during the carrying-out to Right Bn. H.Q. railhead. Coy. proceeded to HILLSIDE SOUTH Camp, S.W. of NEUVE EGLISE, arriving there about 10 P.M.	AL

A. Lomax Capt.
Commanding No. 98 M. G. Coy.

No. 98 MACHINE GUN COY. MACHINE GUN CORPS

CONFIDENTIAL

Vol 19

War Diary
of
98 Machine Gun Company
for
Month of November 1917

Army Form C. 2118.

WAR DIARY
or
INTELLIGENCE SUMMARY.
(Erase heading not required.)

Instructions regarding War Diaries and Intelligence Summaries are contained in F. S. Regs., Part II. and the Staff Manual respectively. Title pages will be prepared in manuscript.

Place	Date Nov 1917	Hour	Summary of Events and Information	Remarks and references to Appendices
NEUVE EGLISE	1		Day was spent in cleaning up after recent trench tour. 2/Lt. F.S.T. ADAMS awarded military cross for gallantry during YPRES operations on 26 Sep. 1917.	A.
do	2.		Coy. inspected at 9.15. belts were cleaned & limbers washed.	A.
do	3		All attached men on range-firing, 9.15 to 2 pm. The O.C., Lt. Sherriff & Obenden, & 2/Lt. Adams reconnoitred ARMENTIERES defences.	A.
do	4		C.of E. & other denominations, parade services.	A.
do	5		Attached and recent draft men on range firing. OC's inspection at 2.15 pm	A.
do	6	7.30 12 noon	B Sec. on range. C Sec. on range. Pte. CHARLES E (88423) reported died of wounds.	A.
do	7	7.30 12 noon	A Sec. on range D Sec. on range 5 O.R. to leave, 5 O.R. returned from leave.	A.

Army Form C. 2118.

WAR DIARY
or
INTELLIGENCE SUMMARY.
(Erase heading not required.)

Instructions regarding War Diaries and Intelligence Summaries are contained in F. S. Regs., Part II. and the Staff Manual respectively. Title pages will be prepared in manuscript.

Place	Date Nov 1917	Hour	Summary of Events and Information	Remarks and references to Appendices
NEUVE EGLISE	8	1 pm	Usual training proceeded with. A Sec moved off to take up AA positions in forward area with artillery. No.70727 Pte. McBride P and No.70332 Pte Campbell D, tried by FGCM for overstaying leave - Sentence, duly promulgated, 3 months F.P. No.1	A1.
do.	9		C. Sec firing on range. Usual training	A1.
do.	10		2/Lt. Bickell reported from leave to U.K. No. 39229 Pte. S. Waring (4th Kings Regt) reported died of wounds 8-10-17	A1.
do.	11	3 pm	Church services for all denominations. A Sec were relieved in AA position by 208 M.G. Coy, & reported back at 6.30 pm	A1.
do.	12	10 AM 1.30 pm	Moved off for MERRIS, via BAILLEUL. Arrived move complete. No. 108674 Pte. YABSLEY died in hospital, 10.11.17.	A1.
MERRIS	13		Inspection of gas appliances & Football inter-section, in the afternoon	A1.

WAR DIARY
or
INTELLIGENCE SUMMARY.
(Erase heading not required.)

Army Form C. 2118.

Place	Date 1917	Hour	Summary of Events and Information	Remarks and references to Appendices
MERRIS	Nov 14		The O.C. reconnoitred line held at PASSCHENDAELE. Usual training carried on. Lieut. W.K. RENNIE, appointed 2nd in command of No. 25 M.G. Coy, left to join unit.	AZ.
do.	15		2/Lt. ARNOTT, C.R., reported from Base Depot. Lieut. W.K.R. AZ. 5 O.R. left for leave to U.K.	AZ.
do.	16	7 AM 7.30 9.0 pm 2.30 4.15 3 pm	Moved off for METEREN. Transport moved off by road for YPRES area. Embussed at METEREN, and proceeded via BAILLEUL & RENINGHELST to YPRES area. Re-bussed 1 mile S.W. of YPRES and marched through YPRES to POTIJZE. Arrived POTIJZE & took up quarters in No. 1 M.G. Camp near cross-roads. Transport arrived by road at POTIJZE	AZ.
POTIJZE	17	AM 9 10.30	Took over accommodation in No. 1 Camp from 14. Canadian M.G. Coy. The O.C. & all available officers reconnoitred positions behind PASSCHENDAELE. No. 29826 Pte. LOMAS, W. sentenced by F.G.C.M. to 3 mths. F.P. No. 1 for Overstaying leave to U.K.	AZ.
do.	18	AM 6.30	Capt. LOMAX left to relieve the Canadian Liaison officer in the line at Bale. H.Q. Preparations made for trench-tour.	AZ.

WAR DIARY
or
INTELLIGENCE SUMMARY.
(Erase heading not required.)

Army Form C. 2118.

Instructions regarding War Diaries and Intelligence Summaries are contained in F.S. Regs., Part II. and the Staff Manual respectively. Title pages will be prepared in manuscript.

Place	Date 1917	Hour	Summary of Events and Information	Remarks and references to Appendices
POTIJZE	Nov 19	AM 5:30	The Coy under Lieut Atherton, left to take over positions in the PASSCHENDAELE sector; proceeded via H & K tracks, north of ZONNEBEKE. D Sec in the village, B Sec holding CREST FARM with two positions in rear; A Sec holding the front of PASSCHENDAELE – BROODSEINDE road, with 2 guns of C Sec in front + 2 in reserve. Coy HQ at TYNE COTTS. B Echelon remains at POTIJZE. Relief complete 10.30 AM. Any remained quiet.	AL
Trenches near PASSCHENDAELE	20		Day was comparatively quiet except for continuous shelling of certain areas, notably CREST FARM and the village. Gas shells near Coy HQ. towards dusk. 1 man gassed. Casualties 1 OR killed, 5 OR wounded (gas poisoning). Harassing fire on Station & MOORSLEDE road carried out at 5.30 pm & 10.30 pm. B Echelon shelled. 1 OR killed, 2 OR wounded, 4 horses killed.	AL
do.	21		Harassing fire as above carried out at 5.30 AM & 11.30 pm. Brick arena shelled between noon & dusk. Otherwise quiet. 5 OR left for leave to UK.	AL
do.	22	6.30 AM 10.0 12 noon 3 pm	Relief by 100th MG Coy began. Relief complete. Quiet relief. Coy proceeded to POTIJZE, No.1 Camp. Capt. LOMAX left Bde HQ being on the Coy. Duties of liaison officer discontinued. Enemy shelled POTIJZE camp. 2 OR killed, 2 OR wounded.	AL
POTIJZE	23		Work begun on site of a new camp N. of POTIJZE – YPRES road.	AL

#353 Wt. W2544/1454 700,000 5/15 D.D. & L. A.D.S.S./Forms/C. 2118.

Army Form C. 2118.

WAR DIARY
or
INTELLIGENCE SUMMARY.
(Erase heading not required.)

Place	Date Nov 1917	Hour	Summary of Events and Information	Remarks and references to Appendices
POTIJZE	24		Work on new camp proceeded with. Transport moved to BUSSEBOOME.	AL
do.	25		Work on new camp proceeded with. Preparation for trench tour.	AL
do	26	3:45 AM	8 detachments, 2 furnished by each section, A+B Secs under 2/Lt. MARSHALL C+D Sec. under Lieut HARTSHORN, moved off under Lieut HEDGELAND to take up Barrage positions in the PASSCHENDAELE sector. Relieved	AL
		7 AM	248 M.G. Coy. A quiet relief & uneventful day. B Echelon at POTIJZE	
1 mile S.W. of PASSCHENDAELE	27		Usual shelling of certain areas along the front, but generally quiet at the barrage positions. Weather fine & dry	AL
do.	28		Nothing of importance at barrage positions. Preparations in hand for providing barrage for 8th Div. attack on our left. Good weather continues.	AL
do	29		Preparations for 8th Div attack continued. About 100,000 rounds placed in position near batteries, shelters for same built & extra barrage positions constructed. Quiet round the position	AL
do	30	6.30 AM	Relieved in barrage positions by No. 100 M.G. Coy. A quiet relief, complete at 8 AM. Proceeded to M.G. camps at POTIJZE on relief.	AL

Cul f. A Thomas Capt.
No. 98 M.G. Coy.

CONFIDENTIAL

V20

War Diary of
98. Machine Gun Company
for Month of December 1917

No. 98 MACHINE GUN COY.
31-12-17
MACHINE GUN CORPS.

Army Form C. 2118.

WAR DIARY
or
INTELLIGENCE SUMMARY.
(Erase heading not required.)

Instructions regarding War Diaries and Intelligence Summaries are contained in F. S. Regs., Part II. and the Staff Manual respectively. Title pages will be prepared in manuscript.

Place	Date 1917 Dec	Hour	Summary of Events and Information	Remarks and references to Appendices
POTIJZE	1		In Divisional M.G. reserve. Work on new camp – drainage &c. Weather mild & dry.	AL.
do.	2		Work on camp improvements. Weather continues good. Back areas around POTIJZE slightly shelled.	AL.
do.	3		Preparations for the trenches – baths, treatment of feet &c.	AL.
Trenches S. of PASSCHENDAELE	4	12:15 AM	Left for the trenches S. of PASSCHENDAELE. Arrived at Coy. H.Q. (TYNE COTT) at 2.30 AM & proceeded to relieve No. 248 M.G. Coy in forward defence positions. Relief complete 7 AM. Dispositions:- "A" Sec. on right (3 positions), B & C Section in centre (6 positions), "D" Sec. on left (2 positions). 2/Lt. F.S.J. ADAMS, M.C. wounded during the relief. Day was fairly quiet after relief but shelling livened up in the afternoon.	AL.
do.	5		Coy. H.Q. heavily shelled during the hours of daylight. Forward positions fairly quiet. S.A.A. taken up by D Sec.	AL.
do.	6		Enemy shelling comparatively light. Good observation positions unmolested. Belt-boxes were taken up to No. 5 position. Forward	AL.
do.	7		Thaw set in & positions became wet and muddy. Heavy shelling of certain areas.	AL.

WAR DIARY
or
INTELLIGENCE SUMMARY.
(Erase heading not required.)

Army Form C. 2118.

Place	Date	Hour	Summary of Events and Information	Remarks and references to Appendices
Trenches S of PASSCHENDAELE	Dec 1917 8	AM 2.30 4.30	No. 100 M.C. Coy. arrived at Coy H.Q. + proceeded to relieve the positions on centre and left (B, C, + D Secs). A quiet relief, complete at 6 AM. Then detachments of No. 146 M.C. Coy arrived + relieved A Sec. in the left AL night positions. Relief complete 6.40 AM. The Coy. proceeded after relief to POTIJZE (camp No.4).	AL
POTIJZE	9		Baths obtained for relieved parts from the trenches. Damp weather prevented work on the camp.	AL
do.	10		Baths for remainder of the Coy. The Coy. was re-equipped from a Divisional pool formed by the M.C. Corps. Lt. C.E. Pritchard reft. from Base Depot.	AL
do.	11	3pm AM 10.30	Lieut. HARTSHORN + 3 O.R. left for course of Anti aircraft at LOVIE aerodrome. Transport arrived from line at BUSSEBOOM.	AL
do.	12		Entrained at St JEAN and proceeded by rail to GODEWAERSVELDE arriving 1pm. By road to billets one mile S.E. of STEENVOORDE. The Coy. occupied three farms - Transport, H.Q. and A+B Secs, and C+D Sections.	AL
Billets near STEENVOORDE	13		Cleaning up clothing and equipment. Committee for sports + other recreational training drew up their	AL

WAR DIARY
or
INTELLIGENCE SUMMARY.
(Erase heading not required.)

Army Form C. 2118.

Instructions regarding War Diaries and Intelligence Summaries are contained in F. S. Regs., Part II. and the Staff Manual respectively. Title pages will be prepared in manuscript.

Place	Date	Hour	Summary of Events and Information	Remarks and references to Appendices
Billets near STEENVOORDE	Dec 1917 14		Guns & gun equipment thoroughly overhauled. No. 70331 Sgt. Harris W. awarded D.C.M. for gallantry in the field. Inter-section football matches on this & every succeeding afternoon. Hard frost set in.	AZ.
do.	15		Limbers washed and S.A.A. in belts changed. Hard frost.	AZ.
do.	16		Church service at EECKE at 10.45 A.M.	AZ.
do.	17		Close order drill & physical drill in the morning. Baths at 12 noon. Frost continues.	AZ.
do.	18		A & B Sections on range. C & D Sections, short route-march via GODEWAERSVELDE. 2/Lt. Marshall + 1 O.R. proceeded on leave to U.K.	AZ.
do.	19		Section training near billets.	AZ.
do.	20		Section training near billets. Frost continues.	AZ.
do.	21	6 AM 9 AM 3.30 pm	C & D Sections on range. A & B Sections, short route-march via GODEWAERSVELDE. Major Gen. Pinney lectured all officers at EECKE on the CAMBRAI battle. Lt. Ockenden attended Court Martial as friend prisoner.	AZ.

WAR DIARY
or
INTELLIGENCE SUMMARY.
(Erase heading not required.)

Army Form C. 2118.

Instructions regarding War Diaries and Intelligence Summaries are contained in F. S. Regs., Part II. and the Staff Manual respectively. Title pages will be prepared in manuscript.

Place	Date	Hour	Summary of Events and Information	Remarks and references to Appendices
Billets near STEENVOORDE	Dec 1917 22		Close-order drill & interior-economy. Frost continues. Lt. Hedgeland + 10 O.R. left for leave to U.K.	AL.
do.	23	12 noon	Distribution of Medal ribbons in G.O.C. 33 Div. at EECKE. 5 O.R. and 2 Officers attended. Ribbons presented to No. 70331. Sgt. Harris W; 11432 Cpl. Bean J; 22848 A/Cpl. Boast R; 70730 L/Cpl. Campbell D.	AL.
		11.45	Church service at EECKE. Lieut. C.S. Hedgeland left on leave to U.K.	AL.
do.	24		Section training in billets. Slight thaw during the day	AL.
do.	25		Christmas Day. Dinner & concert in the company billets	AL.
do.	26		Heavy snow rendered parade impossible. Indoor lectures during morning.	AL.
do.	27		Section parade. Guns calibrated on range near LUMBRES.	AL.
do.	28		Range-practice with revolver & rifle. Snow during afternoon	AL.
do.	29		Interior economy. Lt. Hartshorn ~~and O.R.~~ returned from VIII Corps AA School.	AL.
do.	30		Church service at EECKE.	AL.
do.	31		Coys. Commander lectured Officers & NCO's at STEENVOORDE. Section training near Billets.	AL.

A. Roman Capt.
Commanding No. 98 M.G. Coy.

CONFIDENTIAL
No 21

"War Diary of
98 M.G. Coy for
the Month of January 1918

WAR DIARY
or
INTELLIGENCE SUMMARY.
(Erase heading not required.)

Army Form C. 2118.

Place	Date	Hour	Summary of Events and Information	Remarks and references to Appendices
Billets near STEENVOORDE	Jan 1st 1918		No parades. The men were entertained in the evening by a dinner & concert. Capt. LOMAX left for R.T.C. course at BERTANGLES near AMIENS. Lieut ATHERTON takes over command.	AL
do	2		Section training in the morning. Preparations for leaving the area begun. 2/Lt. C.L. MARSHALL returned from leave to UK.	AL
do	3	AM 6:30	Left to ABEELE where entrained for BRANDHOEK. Arrived in camp about 12.30 pm. Lieut ATHERTON left for leave to UK Lieut T.D. SHERRIFF takes over command.	AL
RIDGE CAMP BRANDHOEK	4	8 AM	Left for POTIJZE (M.G. Camp). Entrained North of BRANDHOEK for YPRES, marched to camp where we arrived about 12.30 p.m. Transport followed by road and arrived in camp shortly about 1 p.m. Fourteen guns teams immediately moved for line and preparations made for same.	PM
M.G. CAMP POTIJZE	5	AM 12:30	Fourteen gun teams left M. Echelon to take up positions (Barrage Lines) in the PASSCHENDAELE Sector of the Line. SHERRIFF in command of group (B) at DAN HOUSE. Lieut T.D. Transport on duty for carrying purposes. Relieved 149th M.G. Coy. Capt. LOMAX returned from R.F.C. at BERTANGLES and takes over command.	PM
"	6, 7, 8		Fourteen gun positions in accordance with D.M.G.O.S M.G. Defence Scheme. Hetchin gun shooting number of each gun and definite positions. Over Rounds Lines of fire were elevation orders as to the duties of each gun i/c. leave to UK attempt positions &c GL 7th Lieut HEDGELAND returns from leave to UK.	PM
"	9		Relieved by No 246 M.G. Coy. Relief complete 3.30 am. Lieut A.W. HARTSHORN Evacuated A/C CAMPBELL and Pte KENT.J wounded on way to A Echelon. 6 am on 10/1/18	PM

WAR DIARY
or
INTELLIGENCE SUMMARY.
(Erase heading not required.)

Army Form C. 2118.

Instructions regarding War Diaries and Intelligence Summaries are contained in F. S. Regs., Part II. and the Staff Manual respectively. Title pages will be prepared in manuscript.

Place	Date 1917 JAN	Hour	Summary of Events and Information	Remarks and references to Appendices
POTIJZE	10		Duty Coys for 4 days. Work on Reserve positions carried on. S.A.A. carried to barrage positions.	AL
	11		The O.C. visited A group H.Q. & arranged details of relief with O.C. 19 M.G. Coy.	AL
	12		Preparation for trench tour. Paraded 11 p.m. & marched to trenches near PASSCHENDAELE.	AL
PASSCHEN-DAELE	13		Relieved 19 M.G. Coy in 9 forward positions. Relief complete 8 A.M. Weather good. Snow on the ground. Enemy artillery inactive. Frost in evening.	AL
	14		Frost continues. Our positions unmolested by hostile artillery. S.A.A. carried up.	AL
	15		Laid guide lines to forward positions N. & S. of PASSCHENDAELE from the main BROODSEINDE road. Snow & sleet at night.	AL
	16		Strong thaw set in. Positions flooded. Conditions very bad. Relieved at 7 p.m. by 248 M.G. Coy & proceeded down to POTIJZE.	AL
POTIJZE	17		Thaw continues. Rest after the trenches. 3 cases trench-foot.	AL
	18		2/Lt. HARRIS, N.A. reported from Base depôt. Lt. OCKENDEN to 21st Squadron R.F.C. on Anti aircraft course.	AL
	19		Fine weather. Work on camp improvements. Lt. Hedgeland reconnoitred barrage positions. Enemy guns active on ST JEAN camp.	AL
	20		Preparation for trenches. Weather fine.	AL

Army Form C. 2118.

WAR DIARY
or
INTELLIGENCE SUMMARY.
(Erase heading not required.)

Instructions regarding War Diaries and Intelligence Summaries are contained in F.S. Regs., Part II. and the Staff Manual respectively. Title pages will be prepared in manuscript.

Place	Date	Hour	Summary of Events and Information	Remarks and references to Appendices
PASCHENDAELE	21		Coy takes over group B (Barrage Positions) from 100th M.G. Coy Lieut RRATHERTON taken to R.F.A.	MEV
"	22		CAPT. A. LOMAX went TO SHERIFFE on leave to U.K. & 3 O.R.'s to U.K. Situation normal. 1/2 firing by barrage guns.	MEV
"	23		Situation normal. 1/2 firing. 2 O.R. Returned to U.K. 1 O.R. from leave to U.K.	MEV
"	24		Lieut R R ATHERTON from R.F.A. 4 O.R's from leave. 15 O.R. 2 O.R's from leave deport. Situation normal. 1/2 firing.	MEV
POTIJZE	25		Coy relieved by 248th M.G. Coy Baths & 2 O.R's transferred from 248th M.G. Coy 3 O.R's from leave to U.K. 1 O.R. killed.	MEV
"	26		ARMY & CORPS Lines accommodated. Cleaning up. 1 parade Lieut J R CKENDEN & 8 O.R's from AHT Coy Self 4 O.R's from leave 1 O.R from A.H.T.D.	MEV
"	27		Packing Limbers. Returned at ST JEAN Steam at 4 p.m. Relieved by 151st M.G. Coy. Arrived ST OMER 9 p.m.	MEV
QUIERCAMP	28		Arrived QUIERCAMP about 12.15 a.m. Inspections	MEV
"	29		General training. 10 O.R. evacuated. 3 O.R's from leave.	MEV
"	30		Inspections relieving guns. 1 O.R. evacuated. Transport arrived.	MEV
"	31		Cleaning guns &c. 2 O.R's from leave.	MEV

C.S. Hedgelands 75th C.G.

www.ingramcontent.com/pod-product-compliance
Lightning Source LLC
Chambersburg PA
CBHW081541160426
43191CB00011B/1812